Becoming a Nurse

A Career Survival Guide

Becoming a Nurse

A Career Survival Guide

Mike Lowry
RGN BEd (Hons) RNT MEd

Senior Lecturer in Nursing
Leeds Metropolitan University
Leeds
England

Kate Taylor
drew the pictures

M Mosby

Copyright © 1993 Mosby–Year Book Europe Limited

Printed and bound in Great Britain by Biddles Ltd, Guildford and King's Lynn

ISBN 0 7234 1926 4

For full details of all Mosby–Year Book Europe Limited titles please write to Mosby–Year Book Europe Limited, Brook House, 2–16 Torrington Place, London WC1E 7LT, England.

A CIP catalogue record for this book is available from the British Library.

Library of Congress Cataloging-in-Publication Data (applied for).

Contents

About The Author

Mike Lowry entered nursing in 1975, following various occupations including motor mechanic, bus driver and car wash attendent. He qualified as a registered nurse and soon after went to Texas, where he worked in a private hospital. On returning to England, he pursued his nursing career in various speciality settings mainly within the National Health Service, and developed an interest in education.

As a mature student he took a degree in education, graduating with first class honours. Two years later, he was awarded a scholarship while working as a university lecturer in Australia, and subsequently obtained his masters degree.

He is presently employed as a senior lecturer in nursing.

He has published widely in professional journals.

Married with 3 children, his hobbies include sport, travel, playing the guitar and writing.

Preface

Despite the thousands of people who for various reasons may come into contact with nurses, it is evident when speaking to lay people and as an educator and admissions tutor, that many harbour false images of what it is to become a nurse. Such impressions may be further distorted where information is out of date, for example from a friend or relative who may have worked as a nurse many years previously.

This book is intended as a guide for those who may be considering a career as a nurse, and will prove useful for existing nursing students as well as registered nurses who are in the early stages of their nursing career. The main issues which are addressed include information on career opportunities in nursing through the various 'branch specialities', details of 'Project 2000' and preregistration nursing degree programmes, how to apply for a place to study, where to apply, and what opportunities await the registered nurse at home and overseas. There is advice on interviews, and surviving living away from home whilst studying. Study skills and exam techniques are also addressed. There is information on what it is like to be newly registered, in the form of vignettes taken from interviews with newly qualified nurses.

Mike Lowry
RGN BEd (Hons) RNT MEd

Acknowledgements

This book is dedicated to Mary, Jennifer, David, Kathryn and to my parents and brother, for their love and support.
To Lawrence for the endless philosophical debates and pints of dark Irish liquid.
My thanks also to Griselda Campbell, Hannah Tudge and Stephen McGrath at Mosby Europe, for always smiling on the telephone.
Finally a special thank you to the students and nurses who embellish these pages.

1

NURSING
MYTH
VERSUS
REALITY

This chapter looks at some common public perceptions of nurses and nursing, and gives a brief history of the profession. There is an analysis of what might constitute a carer, and an opportunity for the reader to assess his or her own potential in this area. Later in the chapter there is a 'snapshot' of what it is like to be a nurse, and a look at the demands and rewards of the job.

STEREOTYPES

Even today, many people imagine a typical nurse to be a woman, who is pretty (but not beautiful), between twenty and thirty years old, and who defers in every way to the doctor (usually a man). Another common image is the provocative and scantily clad siren who teases male patients, male visitors and especially male doctors (who are seen as prospective husbands). The archetypal battle-axe sister has had sufficient airings (in film and TV comedies, on get-well cards etc.) to establish her as an unapproachable dragon, whose words put fear in the hearts of junior doctors and other nurses. Male nurses have not escaped attention, and are often considered to be somehow less masculine, because of their declaration of intent to care. This stereotype, like all the others, can be quickly dismissed— male nurses exhibit the same range of 'masculine' qualities as men in other walks of life.

Media representations of nurses and nursing have helped to construct these stereotypes—a glance through any newspaper will demonstrate the media's liking for easy-to-swallow generalisations— and the public has seemed willing to accept them. Although such stereotypes may, in some cases, contain a grain of truth (despite changes within the profession), most nurses would be quick to dismiss them. The modern nurse is highly skilled, articulate and intelligent, an independent professional in his or her own right.

Much of what the lay person might consider to be a nurse's work (mopping fevered brows, carrying bedpans, awaiting words of wisdom and direction from physicians, and so on) has in the past been the work of women considered incapable or unworthy of other, less 'menial' tasks. In the 17th and 18th centuries, the (stereotypical) nurse was a feeble-minded, gin-soaked woman of easy virtue who had fallen on hard times. Going further back in history it was mainly men, especially those associated with religious/monastic orders, who tended the sick. This group still exists today—nurses of the gin-soaked variety are rather harder to find!

Try This Quiz To See Whether You Are Suited To Nursing

Are you... ?	YES	NO
Someone who enjoys learning	☐	☐
Good at maths, science & English	☐	☐
Able to solve complex problems	☐	☐
Able to keep cool in a crisis	☐	☐
Able to get on with almost everyone	☐	☐
Sensible	☐	☐
A good communicator	☐	☐
Of above average intelligence	☐	☐
Always healthy	☐	☐
Able to manage time easily	☐	☐
Patient, always tolerant of other's faults	☐	☐
Happy to work when friends are at play	☐	☐
A good teacher	☐	☐
Creative	☐	☐
Well liked by those you meet	☐	☐
An excellent judge of character	☐	☐
Very strong willed	☐	☐

Count up your total 'YES' responses. If you scored more than 15, then forget nursing—you should be sitting on a cloud playing a harp, or at least walking about with a halo over your head! Most people who are likely to succeed in nursing should be able to answer 'YES' to a majority of these questions, while recognising their shortcomings and being willing to work on them.

Okay, how does it sound so far?
Are you still interested—are you suited to nursing?

ELEMENTS OF NURSING

Nursing is a very difficult activity to define comprehensively.

Whatever the definition, it will certainly appeal to those seeking a varied occupation which offers considerable scope for individual growth. Personal development begins during preregistration programmes, with the study of interpersonal skills leading to a greater understanding and awareness of self. Added to this is professional and intellectual development through education—the study of a wide range of subjects—and travel, as well as the experience gained in many clinical and non-clinical nursing speciality areas. This description is true of most, if not all, preregistration programmes.

CHARACTERISTICS OF CARERS

It is of little benefit to anyone for a person to enter nursing who does not have a fundamental interest in the care and welfare of others. Nursing is centrally concerned with many issues associated with basic caring (which is, incidentally, anything but basic). Some key characteristics of nurses are listed below.

Common sense—This is not always 'common'!

Empathy—The ability to appreciate how others may be feeling.

Flexibility—The ability to adapt to changing conditions.

A sense of humour—A vital asset in nursing.

Understanding—To care for another person (a patient or client), there must be some understanding of that person's needs. Such understanding calls for self-awareness (of your own strengths and shortcomings), knowledge of a broad range of topics essential to nursing (including science and humanities), and intelligence.

Self-awareness and intelligence—Self-awareness and intelligence are of little use unless they can be applied. A good nurse must have a firm grasp of the theory and, most importantly, must be able to use it to solve often unique and unforeseen problems in a variety of challenging situations, e.g. managing a busy clinical area. It is this ability, to be a 'knowledgeable doer', that separates nurses from many lay people.

Decision making—Nurses face a variety of ethical issues and dilemmas in the course of their daily work: they may have to decide whether to act as an advocate for a patient in their care, perhaps at considerable personal risk; they may have to make difficult decisions concerning patient care, decisions requiring knowledge and under-standing of a number of courses of action. This process may involve other health-care providers and may be complex.

Dealing with complex and demanding situations—Nurses often need to cope with crises which may be physical, emotional or both, and which might involve several people at once. Thus caring may be complex and demanding, even where it may appear at first to be 'basic'. Making it appear basic may be said to be the measure of the true skills of a good nurse.

PERSONAL DEVELOPMENT

Most nurses would agree that they changed, often quite markedly, as they learned how to nurse. Certainly, having to get on with others in a variety of settings makes this kind of personal development possi-ble. The naïve and sometimes idealistic images which one harboured on entering the profession—often the same images employed by the media and enshrined in popular myth—quickly give way to a reality which uncovers personal qualities of which we were previously unaware. Nowhere is this more in evidence than when the nursing student returns home to friends and family, who are always quick to spot the change—all will be eager for you to tell them how you are getting on.

Such change may take several forms, including an increase in your personal confidence, calmness when coping with crises and a heightened awareness of the needs of others. (Your improved listen-ing and attending skills should come into play here.)

You will find that caring has become second-nature ...

THE DEMANDS OF NURSING...

Nursing is often described by lay people as demanding work, the emphasis perhaps being placed on the physical demands. True, the procedural elements of caring may often be physically very tiring and strenuous, but the emotional drains may also be considerable, as you will be involved with people when they are most in need of help. Although nursing students may not be expected to care for others alone and unsupported in clinical areas, and although they enjoy supernumerary status (they are not employed as extra labour, but are in clinical placements to learn), there are certain to be occasions when it all becomes too much. At this stage a good support network of friends, family and working colleagues is important.

The stresses of coping with caring can produce symptoms which manifest as physical or emotional difficulties (for example, aches and pains, frequent colds, loss of energy, weakness, or feeling inexplicably tearful). Early recognition of these symptoms in yourself is essential if treatment within the support network is to be successful. Never forget that you too are human, and are just as likely to be affected by the stresses and strains of nursing as anyone else. Needless to say, the recognition of impending difficulties in others is also important.

At the nursing college or university, students who need help have access to counselling services and to the occupational health department; unfortunately not every student uses these services when he or she should.

...AND THE REWARDS

The notion of reward is interesting, and means something different to each of us—it can take the form of money, the opportunity to work abroad, variety, the intrinsic rewards associated with caring, even glamour!

In the eyes of lay people, the benefits of nursing often focus entirely on the job's vocational elements, something which a nurse is 'drawn to', or 'born to do'. Nurses are seldom associated with high rates of pay, or accorded the status enjoyed by more established professions (such as medicine). Who, for example, ever heard of a wealthy nurse, as opposed to a well-heeled doctor? It is true that nursing is not the quick way to an easy fortune. You will not be lounging on tropical beaches twice a year, unless you happen to work near one.

It is true that the vocational rewards can be immense, but let's be realistic. The professionalism inherent in modern nursing is not arrived at overnight—the skills of nursing take time to develop. Fundamental skills and understanding must be learned; this in itself needs hard work and application by an individual with the intelligence, common sense (for the two do not always go hand in hand)

and tenacity to cope with many and varied demands, in college, at home and in clinical work. The demands of the work call for resources to support them—you will need opportunities to relax and recharge your batteries both physically and emotionally. This in turn requires a decent salary, rather than the subsistence-level payments which student nurses have received in recent years.

In the United Kingdom, the profession attracts salaries which allow nurses to live reasonably well. Indeed, there seems to have been a considerable increase in the number of families whose main wage earner is a nurse. Men and women who in previous years would have been unable to consider supporting a family on a qualified nurse's income may now do so in reasonable comfort. Having said this, most nurses would say that they could do with more money. The salary of a Registered Nurse (*Table 1*) compares with that of a school teacher or a higher grade white collar worker in the civil service. There are opportunities for advancement into very highly paid, though usually non-clinical, posts, but these positions are few and far between, and competition for them is intense.

Rating	Grade	Salary *(per annum)*
Staff nurse	D, E	£10 982–£14 565
Sister/charge nurse	F, G, H	£13 956–£21 010

Table 1   Salaries according to grade (projected 1993 figures, assuming a 1.5% increase from April 1993).

Although pay alone rarely attracts people into nursing, many people find the opportunity of high pay overseas too good to miss. The benefits and disadvantages of this are considered later on (see Chapter 13, *Career Opportunities*).

THE HEALTH SERVICE IN THE 1990s

Changes in the health service in the United Kingdom have implications for those entering and working in the nursing profession. It seems likely that fewer nurses will be employed to deliver 'hands on' care, this being carried out by health-care assistants under qualified nursing supervision. The introduction of self-governing NHS Trust status for many hospitals has led to a change in emphasis, from purely providing health care to providing this in a more commercial and cost-effective way. There is a rapid move towards the development of more Trusts, and this relatively new initiative has met with a mixed response. Some people fear the decline of the health service as it has been known since 1948—others view the changes in a more favourable and positive light.

The proliferation of hospital Trusts is bound to have implications for nurses and nursing. Incomes and career prospects may be affected, as they will no longer be comparable nationally but will vary between different trusts and health authorities. The fact that trusts will endeavour to specialise in the types of service which they offer may lead to a reduction in the variety of clinical experience placements available to nursing students.

SO, WHAT'S IT REALLY LIKE?

Nursing is hard work, few people would deny that. Most nurses are very busy for most of the time, and caring for people in situations where there may not be enough staff or other support tends to be stressful for both individuals and teams of nurses. The foregoing statement may appear negative, but errs on the side of reality in most cases.

On a positive note, it is worth considering nursing not as the task-centred profession it may have been in the past, but more as a multi-faceted set of skills. Such skills consider the needs of the 'whole' person; there can be few more satisfying experiences than establishing a relationship with someone who has come into your care very ill, and in whom you have been able to produce a beneficial change (though not always a cure). An acceptance of your own limitations, coupled with an appreciation of those special qualities and skills which constitute nursing in whatever discipline or speciality area, will make for an ever-increasing breadth of understanding and, in most people, a reinforcement of the desire to nurse.

Snapshots of Nursing Life

Although it is impossible to describe nursing in its entirety, the following 'peep over a nurse's shoulder' should help.
Julie is a recently Registered Nurse:

I remember how I couldn't wait to get home as a student and just put my feet up for half an hour or so, I'd been so busy all day trying to learn new things and look after the patients assigned to me by the staff nurse.... Now I'm in the role of the staff nurse and things have really changed... I have to think so quickly and there are so many demands coming at me from all directions... the 'phone seems to be always ringing, there are other staff to liaise with from everywhere in the hospital including physiotherapists, catering staff, doctors and relatives, as well as the students... I never believed it could be so demanding... but when a patient just looks up, smiles and says 'thank you, that feels much better'... well it just all fits into place somehow, I go home tired but feeling as if I've done something worthwhile... I used to work in an office, but every day seemed the same as the next... nursing is just never boring, you know there is always something new, a fresh challenge... but I still love to get home and take my shoes off!

7

Mark is an experienced charge nurse:

Nursing is all about team work really... you have to work with others—other nurses, other care staff and patients... you need to leave your troubles at home because there isn't space at work to dwell on them... as a charge nurse you need to keep a careful eye out for potential problems both with staff and patients... there is less opportunity for actual 'hands on' patient care but I like to maintain this as much as possible... I used to get ribbed by my friends because I'm a male and I chose nursing, but really caring is just as much for males as females... there is always the opportunity to use your mind in tackling new situations.

KEEPING UP TO DATE

The rapid development of the nursing profession has opened up considerable scope for personal and professional development. Most of the major hospital-based and community health-care services recognise the need for professional development, and most have continuing education departments which offer short courses to staff. The statutory and professional bodies—the United Kingdom Central Council (UKCC) for Nurses, Midwives and Health Visitors, and the national boards for England, Scotland, Northern Ireland and Wales—are beginning to insist on regular programmes of development for all nurses. The Post Registration Education Practice Project (PREPP) requires nurses to complete five days of recognised study every three years, in order to maintain their registration. This is important and relevant given the rapidly changing health care environment of the 1990s. An increasing number of nurses are recognising the need to improve on their basic studies and are seeking higher academic qualifications, enrolling for example on part-time diploma and degree courses. Such development can only improve knowledge and understanding, with benefits for both nurses and patients.

OTHER BENEFITS

A qualified nurse has the opportunity to travel and work in any country or area where there are people in need of care. Indeed, nurses registered since 1983 are fully qualified to work in any EC country. Few other professions offer such flexibility of location, working hours, days or speciality areas. Nurses returning home from overseas placements are not penalised for having left the 'umbrella' of the National Health Service. British employers consider the life and work experience to be beneficial.

The profession is moving forward rapidly. There are considerable opportunities, and whatever you seek in your work you are unlikely to find any to surpass the uniqueness which is nursing.

2

EDUCATION PROGRAMMES EXPLAINED

LEGAL REQUIREMENTS FOR PRACTICE

In the UK, as in most other developed nations, there is a requirement for professionals of all kinds to be controlled by law. Such controls protect the interests of the general public, and allow professionals to practice with the confidence that they act within legally defined boundaries.

Nursing is no exception to this rule. The law in the UK lays down detailed requirements which the trainee must satisfy before he or she can legally act alone (as opposed to acting under supervision, with other professionals ultimately accountable for their actions). The United Kingdom Central Council (UKCC) for Nurses, Midwives and Health Visitors is increasingly responsible for ensuring that the legal requirements are met in the various nursing education programmes, and thus controls how a student may prepare to become a nurse. The UKCC also issues a code of conduct for nurses, midwives and health visitors, which gives qualified nurses guidance in carrying out their work.

LEGAL REQUIREMENTS FOR EDUCATION

The minimum amount of study which must be completed in a pre-registration programme is 4600 hours, this being a mixture of practical- and theory-based study. A full-time, college-based course usually takes three years; degree courses take three or four years, depending on the institution. All must fulfil minimum requirements in terms of theory and the amount and type of clinical experience.

Within the definition of the term 'nurse' there is a subtle but important issue, in that many people without formal qualifications do call themselves nurses. However, under the terms of the Nurses, Midwives and Health Visitors Act 1979, only those who have successfully completed an approved programme may legally use the title 'Registered Nurse'.

Since 1st September 1992, all qualified nurses have used the title Registered Nurse, with the abbreviation 'RN'. They must specify which part of the register they appear on when applying for jobs. Those who are presently on level 1 of the register (i.e. those who registered following a minimum of 4600 hours' preparation) will be distinguished from those who were previously known as 'enrolled nurses', by the part of the register on which they are recorded.

An approved programme is one which is offered by an institution, allied to a clinical experience circuit in one or more hospitals and community service areas. The institution may be a college of nursing or of Health, or may be a department in a larger institution, such as a university. Colleges of nursing share clinical experience placements, and staff may contribute to teaching on each other's courses. Examples of available courses include:

- 'Traditional' courses.
- Project 2000—planned to replace traditional courses.
- Nursing degree programmes.
- Enrolled nurse (level 2) conversion to registration (level 1).

More information about these courses is available in later chapters. Having considered the basic outline requirements for becoming a nurse, we can now consider specific courses leading to registration. The information in this section applies only to those who already have the enrolled nurse qualification.

ENROLLED NURSES—CONVERSION TO REGISTRATION
The enrolled nurse (level 2) qualification has in the past offered an alternative route to a career in nursing. The qualification, two years in duration, was largely vocational and had a relatively low theoretical content. Such programmes are no longer offered in the UK.

There are many thousands of practising enrolled nurses whose career prospects are limited due to the restrictions imposed by their qualification. Many of these extremely competent and experienced practitioners may wish to convert their qualification to registrationin order to develop their career and professional opportunities, and their management and planning skills.

There are three ways for enrolled nurses to convert to registration. All require hard work and commitment, not only while studying but also just to get on the course. The number of places is limited, particularly for full-time courses, and demand is always high.

Full-time Conversion
These one-year programmes are run by approved colleges of nursing. Most students on this type of programme are seconded by their employer, and are paid as an enrolled nurse on their existing grade

throughout the period of study. The course is intensive and lasts for twelve months, although it may be possible to negotiate some advance standing if the student has other appropriate qualifications, for example completion of certain relevant courses offered by the Open University. Precise details of which courses may be considered appropriate will be held by the course tutor. Competition for places is fierce, and applicants should ensure that they have evidence of recent study, such as short courses run through the Open University, or GCSE/A levels. An application which lacks evidence of recent study is unlikely to impress tutors—carefully planned study leading up to the time of application will greatly help both your application and your confidence.

Flexible Part-time Conversion
These part-time, distance learning programmes are affiliated to existing colleges of nursing and usually take about two years to complete. The course is pursued in the student's own time. Some work is done alone, and some in 'tutor groups', each group having its own Registered Nurse as tutor. It is essential that applicants are employed for the equivalent of at least half full-time in a nursing post. This should ensure that the student receives the appropriate number of hours of clinical learning, as opposed to clinical work which has no educational emphasis. Unlike the full-time programme, it is not essential to furnish evidence of recent study although, as a run-up to such a course, some recent study would undoubtedly help. These programmes enable the student to work and study as and when it is convenient, an asset to those with family responsibilities or other commitments. Fees are normally paid by the student—the total cost over two years leaves little change from £2000.

Nursing Degree
The third option for enrolled nurses is to undertake a full-time degree in nursing, with registration. As an undergraduate, the enrolled nurse follows exactly the same programme as others on the course. (There is unlikely to be any chance of advance standing, as the level of study on the degree is way beyond that covered in enrolled nurse programmes.) Some enrolled nurses do take this route, although they are at present in the minority. It is advisable to have studied at GCSE/A level or equivalent. Indeed, many admissions tutors will expect you to have such qualifications as you may find it difficult to keep up with the course if the subjects are completely new and unfamiliar. (Bear in mind that your fellow students have probably studied at this level quite recently.) You should find the lecturers encouraging and supportive, but they certainly won't do the course for you.

Undergraduate nursing courses vary in their emphasis, so arm yourself with good advice. Before applying for a course, arrange an informal interview with the admissions tutor, or with one of the course lecturers. If you consider all this a bit too much, remember that other enrolled nurses have succeeded in obtaining nursing degrees. You will have the advantage of maturity and motivation over your 18- to 20-year-old peers, which goes a long way towards success.

Financing the Degree Course

Students on this type of programme normally qualify for a mandatory grant, and as an enrolled nurse you may be able to supplement this through part-time work. The grant is awarded through your local education authority. As each individual case differs from the next, it is recommended that you contact your authority for an assessment of your entitlement. Further details are given elsewhere (see Chapter 5, *Nursing Degrees*).

SUMMARY

- In order to be able to practise legally as a Registered Nurse, a person must satisfy certain requirements, in terms of both type and amount of nursing experience gained.
- Enrolled nurses (level 2) may convert their qualification to level 1 registration by various routes: a flexible part-time conversion; a full-time conversion; a full-time undergraduate degree programme.
- The changing health needs of the population (e.g. the increase in community health care required by an increasingly elderly population) has called for a new approach to nursing education.

PROJECT 2000

3

A NEW APPROACH

Traditional nursing education has focused on the acquisition of task-oriented, rather than problem-solving, skills. It is argued that this approach has produced nurses who are unable or unwilling to generate change by a process of problem solving, so that established working practices are continued even when they are not the most efficient, or are no longer appropriate. Furthermore, nurses as a group have been rather reluctant to speak out on what they see as the profession's needs, preferring to take their lead from other professions, notably medicine. Project 2000 (also known as P2K) has developed with these criticisms in mind, and emphasises the development of interpersonal skills, assertiveness and problem-solving, rather than task-centred training.

This new approach to nurse education has, perhaps inevitably, attracted criticism. Much has been said about P2K, expressing a range of concerns which include fears that new practitioners may be unable to cope with the 'real world' of nursing, that the increased theoretical content will not help the practitioner to perform actual patient care, and that the programme will produce nurses who are lazy and lack the motivation to care or to carry out 'hands on' tasks.

Although there may be a few nurses who fit these descriptions, many of the criticisms raised are the result of an understandable resistance to what is a quite fundamental change in educational practice. For some there is the perceived threat to their career prospects by the 'new' nurses, who will have an academic advantage; others may suffer feelings of inadequacy in the face of the increased knowledge base and, perhaps, the ability to argue from a more enlightened standpoint. Whatever the reasons for resistance (and there is no shortage of this), the new programme is here to stay. All nurse basic preparation in the UK will be changed to Project 2000 in the early 1990s, and traditional courses have already been phased out completely in many places.

BURSARY

Students on Project 2000 programmes get a tax-free bursary (*Table 2*), the starting amount varying according to age and, in some cases, number of dependents. For the purposes of Project 2000 bursaries, students over the age of 26 years are 'mature'.

Age	Bursary payment *(per annum)*
Under 26 years old	£4320
26 years old or over	£4860

Table 2 Bursaries for Project 2000 students (March 1993).

STUDENT UNIONS

Membership of the National Union of Students (NUS) is available to Project 2000 students. This confers benefits unavailable to traditional nursing students, e.g. use of some higher education facilities, discounts in local and national shops, and travel and insurance services.

ENTRY REQUIREMENTS

Requirements for Project 2000 programmes are broadly similar to those for traditional courses—5 subjects at GCE O level/GCSE Grade C or equivalent. Other qualifications, e.g. British Technical and Education Council (BTEC), will also be considered. Those applicants not in possession of these qualifications may in some cases satisfy the entry requirements by sitting an entrance examination.

In addition to the basic entry qualifications outlined above, higher qualifications, e.g. GCE A levels, may in practice be required by many colleges. Some applicants already have a degree on entry. Applications are made through the Nurses and Midwives Central Clearing House (NMCCH) (see Appendix, *Useful Addresses*).

There are significant differences between traditional and Project 2000 programmes, particularly where student clinical placements are concerned, and also at the level of theory and how it is taught.

SUPERNUMERARY STATUS

Students attending clinical placements have supernumerary status. In the past they were included in the numbers of staff on a duty roster, and thus given tasks which may have had very questionable educational benefits. Supernumerary status is intended to ensure that students are not seen as part of the work force, and are not used as cheap labour on the wards. Students on the Project 2000 programme are allocated to clinical areas to observe and participate in the most educationally beneficial way.

COURSE STRUCTURE

Preregistration programmes are legally required to give students a minimum of 4600 hours of theoretical and clinical education. The basic structure of Project 2000 courses is such that all students, regardless of ultimate branch choice, share a Common Foundation Program (CFP) which takes 18 months to complete. In the CFP, core areas of theory are addressed. Clinical placements in branches other than the student's main branch choice give a broad awareness of nursing environments. For example, students in the mental health branch will get some experience in children's nursing, and so on.

The CFP is followed by a branch programme appropriate to the student's chosen speciality area. Applicants have to choose one of four available speciality branch areas at the beginning of the course:

- Adult General Nursing.
- Paediatric/Sick Children's Nursing.
- Mental Health Nursing.
- Mental Handicap Nursing. (Also known as 'learning difficulties'.)

The branch programme lasts a further 18 months, making a total of three years for the entire course up to registration (*Table 3*).

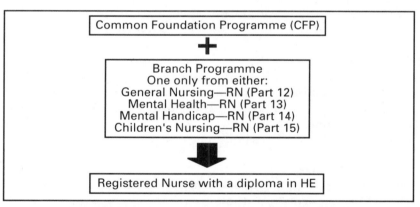

Table 3 Structure of Project 2000. (Numbers in brackets indicate appropriate parts of the professional register.

TOPICS WHICH MAY BE STUDIED IN PROJECT 2000

The teaching style for Project 2000 is a more student-directed approach, following a higher education model. Staff expose students to issues using a variety of media, including seminars, tutorials and lectures; the students then explore these issues in greater depth both individually and in groups. The didactic information-giving style of the traditional course is less in evidence, giving way to a more exploratory approach.

The student follows six major themes in the CFP. An outline of these areas of study is given below.

- BIOLOGY—anatomy, physiology, biochemistry, and the structure and function of the human body.
- SOCIOLOGY—how people live in society, and the effects of the environment on health and welfare.
- HEALTH—nutrition, exercise and lifestyles, and how these may be used to promote health.
- PSYCHOLOGY—study of the mind, normal function and theories from the various schools of psychology.
- INTERPERSONAL SKILLS—learning about oneself and others, to improve interactions with those for whom we care.
- NURSING—caring skills, which may be both 'hands on' skills and the theories of nursing which guide practice.

The study of these core areas gives a foundation for specialised study in the student's chosen branch area. It emphasises the need for an awareness of oneself and of others. Indeed, many students find that they grow most noticeably and most rapidly in self-awareness and in interpersonal studies. This area of enquiry, which many find new and rather daunting, lets students explore elements of their personalities in a controlled, sensitive way, giving a greater understanding of themselves, and thus of those for whom they are to care.

THE CLINICAL EXPERIENCE
Because nursing means caring for people in a variety of settings, experience is gained both in hospitals and in the wider community. The student will of course be expected to wear a uniform when appropriate. Some will find this more acceptable than others, which isn't surprising given the unappealing design of some uniforms!

The Clinical Supervisor
Each student in clinical placement is assigned a clinical supervisor, who will be an experienced Registered Nurse. The pair will work together in delivering care and exploring issues relevant to that care. Students may find themselves in new situations almost weekly, given the unique layout of the Project 2000 programme—visits to each clinical area last initially for just a few days, and build up to several weeks at a time. An ability to adapt to new situations is of paramount importance, and becomes a part of the learning process. However, at no time should students find themselves in a clinical situation for which they are unprepared and in which they are unsupported by a Registered Nurse. Any students who do feel that they are unsupported should discuss this with their supervisor, or contact their tutor at the school or college of nursing.

A TYPICAL WEEK IN THE PROJECT 2000 PROGRAM

Curricula vary from one college to the next, so what follows is an example of what a Project 2000 student might reasonably expect to encounter.

A typical week in the CFP, Monday to Friday, may have anything from two to seven hours of classroom contact or independent study per day, interspersed with periods of clinical experience in a hospital or community area. The ratio of classroom to clinical experience varies from college to college, and depends on the student's place in the programme. For example, a recent starter may spend more time in the classroom learning theory than someone towards the end of the CFP, who is concentrating on gaining clinical experience. Be prepared to spend several months in class before you have much contact with patients—many students find this a shock as well as a source of frustration.

The branch programmes give the student in-depth experience of the clinical work relevant to his or her chosen speciality area, with appropriate theoretical support from the college environment. You have already seen that the theoretical curriculum is broad and varied. It should integrate at each stage with other subjects.

UPON COMPLETION OF THE COURSE

Upon successful completion of the clinical and theoretical components of the course, students are granted Registered Nurse status in their chosen speciality area, and receive a Diploma in Higher Education. At this stage you are legally entitled to call yourself a Registered Nurse, and to work as such. Registered Nurses are legally and professionally responsible for their actions, and may be disciplined for misconduct by the UKCC—serious cases of misconduct may lead to the nurse being removed from the register and thus legally prevented from practising.

Some may wish to convert their diploma into a degree in nursing. Those wishing to study for a degree in another discipline may do so using the Credit Accumulation Transfer Scheme (CATS). CATS is operated by the various National Boards and allows students to put existing study credits (e.g. from a diploma) towards a degree in another discipline (see Chapter 14, *Education and Academia*). In terms of branch choices in nursing, some may wish to pursue study in another speciality; facilities may exist to complete another branch programme over a period of 18 months or less.

The Project 2000 programme satisfies all the requirements of the European Community (EC). Nurses registered through Project 2000 are therefore immediately qualified to work in all EC member states. Employment in non-EC states is also possible (see Chapter 13, *Career Opportunities.*)

ADVANTAGES AND DISADVANTAGES OF PROJECT 2000 COURSES

Money
For many entrants to nursing, money is not the main consideration. Nevertheless, the Project 2000 bursary is lower than the salary of the traditional student, whose pay attracts supplements for unsocial working hours. However, the latter must pay income tax and national insurance contributions, whereas the Project 2000 student gets a tax-free bursary and is exempt from paying council tax. Once these factors are considered, the two payments work out about the same.

Knowledge Base
The increased breadth and depth of theory studied in the Project 2000 programme is advantageous, given the need for future nurses to have more theoretical knowledge and understanding. It is also beneficial for nursing as a profession. However, those students who are less interested in theory and who wish to get more 'hands on' nursing experience may become frustrated at having to wait so long—up to eight months in the CFP—before they can work directly with patients.

However, nurses registered on Project 2000 programmes do satisfy all the legal and professional requirements, and are just as proficient as those qualifying through the traditional route. There should be no doubt whatsoever about the competence of Project 2000-prepared nurses.

Working Conditions
There is little shift work in the early parts of the course, which gives a stability which many students prefer.

Furthermore, the amount of time devoted to self-directed learning gives students on Project 2000 programmes considerably greater personal freedom.

Prospects
The qualification—a Diploma rather than a Certificate—will no doubt be attractive. It should improve short-term employment prospects, and smooth the path for those who wish to enter degree programmes later on in their careers.

As well as the advantages of having a diploma, there are benefits for those wishing to work overseas in countries whose nurses are educated to diploma level.

SUMMARY

- Project 2000 is a new approach to preregistration preparation, emphasising a student-directed problem-solving approach to learning, rather than the didactic 'chalk and talk' approach used in previous courses.

- The academic level of Project 2000 courses is higher than traditional courses, but not as high as degree programmes.

- The successful student will emerge as a Registered Nurse with a diploma in higher education.

- The first half of the course is called the Common Foundation Program (CFP). It takes 18 months to complete and is followed by all students, regardless of branch speciality.

- In the second half of the course students concentrate on their chosen speciality. These branch programmes also take 18 months to complete. There are four branches offered as special areas of study, the same as those offered for traditional programmes:
  Adult General Nursing RN (Part 12).
  Mental Health Nursing RN (Part 13).
  Mental Handicap Nursing RN (Part 14).
  Paediatric/Sick Children's Nursing RN (Part 15).

- There are periods of clinical experience over the three years, in which all students sample work in specialist areas other than their main branch choice. In the early stages of the programme clinical exposure is less than on traditional courses, but increases as the programme progresses.

- Students registered through these programmes may practice nursing in the European Community member states.

4

TRADITIONAL REGISTRATION PROGRAMMES

Until very recently, so-called traditional programmes were the most common way to obtain registration as a nurse. These courses involve three years of full-time study and contain a mixture of theoretical and practical work, following a structure which is similar throughout the UK. The theory is studied in a college of nursing, and the practical experience is gained in a variety of clinical settings. Traditional programmes emphasise practical nursing and are offered through nursing colleges affiliated to hospitals and community care services.

Although some colleges of nursing continue to offer traditional courses, most are introducing Project 2000 courses (see Chapter 3).

BRANCHES OF NURSING
Although the emphasis is on caring for the 'whole person' and not just the illness, nursing is divided into four main branches (see below). Each student selects just one of these as their main branch area, at the beginning of the course. Whatever a student's main branch choice, the programme will nevertheless include periods of study and experience in other areas. Traditional programmes offered by colleges of nursing are:

• Registered General Nurse (RGN) or RN (Part 1).
• Registered Mental Nurse (RMN) or RN (Part 3).
• Registered Sick Children's Nurse (RSCN) or RN (Part 8).
• Registered Nurse Mental Handicap (RNMH) or RN (Part 5).

Registered General Nurse (RGN)
This is the branch area in which the largest numbers of students choose to study, as the demand for RGNs is greater than that for other other branches.

Students completing this programme are employed in 'general' hospital or community settings, caring for people who have, or are recovering from, a physical illness. The areas in which students find themselves working vary from long-stay hospital wards to acute admission, from operating theatres to intensive care areas. During this time the student is assigned to a Registered Nurse in the area, and works closely with that person.

The role of the community nursing practitioner is increasingly important (moves are afoot to enable them to prescribe drugs) as more and more people are cared for in the community rather than in a hospital. Students spend some time experiencing the work of community-based nurses. They accompany the nurse on visits to patients in their homes, as well as observing clinic work at health centres.

Registered Mental Nurse (RMN)

Registered Mental Nurses are employed in long- and short-term 'psychiatric' hospital or community settings, caring for people who have, or are recovering from, a mental illness. As with general nursing, students work with a Registered Nurse, and they care for patients together. A great many people need care for mental health problems at some point in their lives, whether it is in hospital or in the community; students experience acute and long-stay settings, where the emphasis is on helping patients to care for themselves through rehabilitation programmes. Trainees study psychology, interpersonal skills and counselling as essential components of their course, as well the uses of pharmacology in mental health care.

The pace of work in mental health settings is often much more relaxed than in general nursing. It may take some considerable time for the nurse to establish a 'safe' relationship with the patient in order to gain trust and assist in care. Patients, or clients as they are sometimes called, experience a variety of mental health problems; some are relatively short-lived, and others are deep-seated and quite profound. The nurse works very closely with individuals, building up a trusting relationship and ultimately providing support through the period of illness, as well as continuity of care through liaison with community-based nurses.

There is a steady demand for nurses with this qualification, and individuals may find prospects for working as practitioners in the community increasing in line with changes in the health-care system. There is also the opportunity to specialise as a nurse therapist, by taking a special course of study after registration.

Registered Sick Children's Nurse (RSCN)

Students completing this programme are employed in 'general' hospital or community settings caring for sick children. The work is very varied, and ranges from caring for children suffering from infectious diseases, through to intensive care of newborn children. A large part of this work involves the families of the children who are being cared for, so a wide range of interpersonal skills is required. As well as caring directly for sick children, these nurses are also health educators to the parents and families.

There is often a shortage of highly skilled nurses in this area, especially in high-dependency areas such as intensive care of newborn babies—such skills are therefore often in great demand.

Registered Nurse Mental Handicap/Learning Difficulties (RNMH)
Students completing this programme are employed in hospital or community settings, caring for people who have a mental handicap (increasingly known as 'learning difficulties').

Nursing those with a mental handicap (or learning difficulty) calls for patience, tact and understanding. It includes caring for those whose handicaps are mentally and physically profound and who have to remain in hospital, through to those who are learning to live in the wider community. The nurse therefore needs a broad range of skills, combining a measure of general nursing expertise with a deep understanding of the emotional and intellectual needs of both the patients and their families. Some patients may exhibit profound disturbances or challenging behaviour, calling for special skills in their care.

This is the smallest in number of the four branches, and the work is highly specialised. Long-term relationships with clients and their families are a feature of this branch of nursing.

DUAL QUALIFICATIONS
Some nurses find an interest in other branches of nursing, and may wish to develop further in these areas.

In the traditional system it is possible for a nurse who has completed one of the above courses and who wishes to further her or his studies, to complete a shortened course and obtain a dual qualification. The shortened course usually takes half the time needed for initial registration; registration as an RGN takes about three years, whereas the addition of an RMN qualification would take just eighteen months. Places are limited and are in demand. As Project 2000 courses become more established, there will be opportunities for existing Registered Nurses to study for alternative registrations through another (further) branch programme.

Students taking post-registration courses have in the past received exactly the same pay as staff nurses. It is not clear whether this pay structure will continue as self-governing trusts become more common.

There are also opportunities for Registered Nurses to extend their skills into such areas as midwifery, community practice, health visiting and others. (See Chapter 13, *Career Opportunities*.)

Details of institutions offering shortened post-registration courses can be obtained from the National Boards of England, Scotland, Wales and Northern Ireland (see Appendix, *Useful Addresses*).

Of course, a patient's illness will not necessarily fit neatly into the category defined by your branch specialisation. A nurse in any area may find herself involved in caring for people with a mixture of needs, for example when a patient with a mental handicap/learning difficulty is admitted to a general hospital for an operation.

PAY FOR STUDENTS

Students on traditional registration programmes receive a non-means-tested allowance which is treated as a salary and is, therefore, taxable. The allowance increases according to the year in which the student is on the course (*Table 4*).

Student Year	Salary (**per annum**)
1	£6820
2	£7200
3	£7900

Table 4 'Traditional' nursing student salaries (March 1993).

This basic pay is increased if unsocial hours are worked (shifts outside of 'normal' working hours/days) or if clinical experience is carried out in areas where all staff receive enhancements (e.g. caring for patients who are mentally ill). Nursing students on traditional programmes are treated as salaried employees, and do not enjoy full 'student' status.

ENTRY REQUIREMENTS

Applications must be made through the Nurses and Midwives Central Clearing House (NMCCH), details of which are in the Appendix (*Useful Addresses*). Applications made through NMCCH follow a strict timetable (see Chapter 7, *Applying for Places*).

Age Requirements

Age on entry must be at least 17½years, and is negotiable in the upper age range (students over 50 are not unknown). Most admissions tutors would consider life- and work-experience to be an asset.

Health Requirements

Good health is an important requirement for all preregistration nursing programmes. Candidates must be able to meet the physical and emotional demands which the course will make. There are often health screening and immunisation requirements, details of which may be obtained through the nursing college. It is worth mentioning here that applicants with some types of health disorders (e.g. controlled diabetes, epilepsy) may still be considered, provided they can demonstrate that their health is sufficiently good to meet the demands of the job.

Academic Requirements

The academic requirement for traditional courses is usually five passes at GCSE or equivalent. 'Equivalent' qualifications include Business and Technical Education Council (BTEC) courses, and further education 'access to nursing' courses, offered through local Further Education (FE) colleges. Where competition for places is high, institutions may expect more than the stated minimum qualifications.

Those without the minimum passes may be able to sit an entrance test as an alternative route of entry. This route is most commonly taken by mature entrants who have left secondary education with few or no qualifications. The test is intended to assess an applicant's skills in reasoning, numeracy and literacy. It is worth noting here that the academic background of applicants varies enormously, from those without any qualifications whatsoever, to those who possess a university degree. Age is not necessarily a barrier—older candidates may have advantages over their school-leaver counterparts in terms of maturity and motivation, making them attractive to admissions tutors. Many excellent applicants begin their nursing training having spent years in other careers or bringing up a family.

The personal qualities of applicants are ranked very highly and are keenly assessed by interviewers, as is evidence of motivation to do the course, and insight into what may be involved in the course and in nursing.

STRUCTURE OF TRADITIONAL COURSES

The main emphasis of traditional programmes is to provide the student with a broad practical understanding of a nurse's main remit—caring for patients in a practical way in a variety of clinical situations. The practical components of the course typically last eight-to-twelve weeks each; shorter periods in the classroom cover human biology, psychology, social studies, pharmacology (drugs and their uses) and information related to the next area of clinical experience (e.g. surgical nursing for those following a general nursing programme, a specific mental health area for those following a psychiatric nursing programme, and so on). Clinical experience generally includes shift work (early-morning start, late-evening finish and weekend work) whereas college-based study does not (*Table 5*).

The style of teaching is largely traditional. Tutors deliver information to the class who can (in theory) then go away and read more about the conditions experienced by patients. This prepares students for the types of task which they might reasonably be expected to carry out in clinical settings.

ASSESSMENTS

In addition to formal exams and continuously assessed coursework such as projects and essays, students are assessed by tutors or other appropriately qualified clinical staff (Registered Nurses) in order to determine their competence in clinical areas. There are several pieces of assessed work over the three years of the course. A student who fails to complete an assessment may become ineligible for registration as a nurse, and would therefore have to leave the course.

The academic content of this type of programme is necessarily basic, having certificate status in the hierarchy of qualifications. However, the course does attract a credit rating under the Credit Accumulation Transfer Scheme (CATS). (For further information see Chapter 14, *Education and Academia*.)

ADVANTAGES AND DISADVANTAGES OF TRADITIONAL COURSES

A major advantage of the traditional route is that students are able to work with patients very early on, sometimes just eight weeks into the introductory period. Many students find this very attractive, as it fulfils their desire to help the sick and allows them to work with the professional nurses to whose positions they aspire. Another advantage is the pay, which can be increased if unsocial hours are worked.

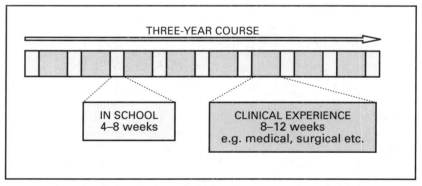

Table 5 Sample structure of a traditional course totalling three years. This work schedule is interspersed with annual leave, public holidays and days off. (Details differ between institutions.)

A disadvantage of this system is that busy clinical staff may see a student as little more than an extra pair of hands, suitable only for simple, low-status jobs (with more technical tasks reserved for the Registered Nurse). In times past, this nursing hierarchy was strictly enforced—not so long ago, trainees would have to open the door for students just one or two years their senior, and wouldn't dare to sit at the same dining table as a sister or staff nurse. Although some of these distinctions still exist, much unnecessary pettiness has, thankfully, disappeared. Nevertheless, one nursing sister admits to having had students push her along the ward in a laundry basket! Strange, but true. I still recall another nursing sister, as recently as 1981, who said that she considered students to be her slaves!

The traditional training methods have been stoutly defended, for the most part by nurses who are themselves products of that system. Some see the new courses as a threat to their career prospects. In fact, Registered Nurses who have taken care to further their skills and education should have little to fear.

In spite of the opposition, the traditional route is being phased out in favour of Project 2000, which gives more academic credibility to nursing and approaches the preparation of nurses in a very different way (see Chapter 3, *Project 2000*).

Traditional courses give the student an early opportunity to experience the realities of clinical work...

SUMMARY

- Traditional programmes leading to registration emphasise a practical approach, with limited theoretical coverage.

- There are four branches to choose from, leading to specialisation areas:

General nursing	RGN or RN (Part 1)
Mental health nursing	RMN or RN (Part 3)
Mental handicap nursing	RNMH or RN (Part 5)
Sick children's nursing	RSCN or RN (Part 8)

- Each programme comprises 4600 hours of theory and practice.

- Nursing students on traditional programmes receive a salary.

- The minimum age on entry to a programme is $17\frac{1}{2}$ years, with no specified upper age limit.

- The number of places on traditional programmes is decreasing, as more and more colleges adopt Project 2000.

5

NURSING DEGREES

Nursing as an academic discipline is moving forward rapidly, and as such offers plenty for even the most enquiring mind. Nursing can be studied at all academic levels including Bachelor's, Master's and Doctoral programmes (for more information see Chapter 14, *Education and Academia*).

It is possible to embark on a combined programme, leading to registration as a nurse and a degree in nursing. This is very demanding, as it involves study for both an academic and a vocational qualification. Such degree programmes do not always offer a wide choice of branch speciality, and some offer only general nurse registration (see Appendix, *Useful Addresses*).

The length of time needed to complete the degree varies between institutions, and may be either three or four years in total. Such courses are offered by institutions of higher education, i.e. universities, whether long-standing or recently-created (from the old polytechnics). These courses are well established, and equip graduates to work as well-qualified practitioners with, some argue, a head start in the employment market. Undergraduates on nursing degrees have the same status as other university students. However, because the course compresses a full degree and the equivalent of a three-year registration programme into just three or four years' study, the workload is heavy and the holidays shorter than those enjoyed by students on many other undergraduate courses. Nursing degrees usually take more than 41 weeks per year, as opposed to 36 weeks or less with non-nursing courses.

A mandatory grant is available for all undergraduates, although many (if not all) students would argue that it is grossly inadequate. Many are forced to take part-time jobs in order to survive. University students can of course join the National Union of Students (NUS) which has some associated benefits, such as discounts in some shops, and student travel concessions.

STRUCTURE

The structure of degree programmes varies; specific information on course structure should be sought from individual institutions. All cover similar topic areas to Project 2000 programmes, but in greater depth. An example of one possible combined registration/degree course is outlined below.

Year 1

Study of people and their health needs, focusing on health in the community but with some visits to hospitals and domestic settings. Theory includes study of anatomy, physiology, psychology, sociology, pharmacology, microbiology, biochemistry and possibly others, so there won't be much free time.

Year 2

Study of people from childhood to old age, with clinical experience in appropriate hospital and community settings. Theory as year one, but in greater depth (*Table 6*).

TERM 1	TERM 2	TERM 3
children's nursing associated theory	adult nursing associated theory	elderly care associated theory

Table 6 Example of undergraduate programme, year 2.

Year 3

'High-level' experience, e.g. in accident/emergency, acute mental health and intensive care. Several weeks of clinical placement in each setting together with relevant theory.

Year 4

Consolidation of previous three years' study, with research experience and more on the role of staff nurses. There may be clinical placements, in some instances in areas selected by the students themselves. Some students find this year a useful introduction to their first post as a staff nurse.

ASSESSMENTS

The workload is continuous and demanding, with essays, projects, seminars, exams and research assessed at various stages throughout the programme.

All must comply with the minimum 4600 hours of theory and clinical practice required for traditional and Project 2000 programmes. The early and mid-1990s will see more Project 2000-type degree courses, in which all students follow a common foundation programme and then choose a branch programme. One major difference between the two courses remains, namely the academic depth to which the various subjects are studied. Although Project 2000 courses cover theory in greater depth than traditional programmes, degrees will continue to demand an even deeper understanding in all subject areas.

Undergraduate programmes place great emphasis on self-direction and the development of the student's intellectual skills to an advanced level, and many courses culminate in a major research project or proposal in the final year.

ADVANTAGES AND DISADVANTAGES

The numbers of nursing graduates looks set to increase, with degrees becoming a requirement for many senior posts in the profession. The numbers of undergraduates currently studying means that students are likely to work and study in relatively small groups, with the advantage that they can get to know their teachers well. As with Project 2000 courses, undergraduates are supernumerary and are put on clinical placements for strictly educational purposes. But it is very hard work!

ENTRY REQUIREMENTS

Good health is important, as nursing is very demanding. You may have to undergo a medical examination prior to taking up a place on the course, and you will certainly need to produce evidence of immunisation against such conditions as hepatitis and tetanus.

ACADEMIC REQUIREMENTS

In common with the majority of undergraduate programmes, the academic requirements are usually two or three passes at GCE A level or equivalent, although the pass grade varies between institutions. As with the other programmes, there are alternative routes of entry. These include British Technical and Education Council (BTEC) qualifications, and other non-standard access courses. For some mature candidates, personal qualities and previous work experience may be considered a fair measure of their likely success on the course. It is worth noting that high A-level grades do not always guarantee success on degree programmes; in fact, the reverse is sometimes the case. Even so, there are generally many more applicants than there are available places—it is not unusual for an admissions tutor to receive 800 or more applications each year for just 30 places—and competition can be fierce.

Applications for full-time degree programmes must be made through central clearing systems which coordinate applications nationally. These are PCAS for the new universities (recently created from polytechnics), and UCCA for the older universities. The two are set to combine in 1994, after which applicants will apply through just the one clearing system (see Appendix, *Useful Addresses*).

UPON COMPLETION OF THE COURSE

Successful students are granted Registered Nurse status, together with an honours or a pass degree. Graduate status implies more than just a possible boost in employment prospects—the intellectual development which takes place brings many rewards on a personal level, both in and out of work. Graduates usually find that their intellectual and critical abilities have developed considerably as a result of their course.

Most nursing graduates opt to work in clinical rather than academic settings, which runs counter to the notion held by some people: that graduates always go straight into management, research or teaching.

Nursing has not yet recognised the benefits of graduates in terms of financial rewards, so a graduate cannot expect any extra pay for the effort of obtaining a degree. This is interesting when compared to school teachers, for example, whose academic success is reflected in their starting pay!

SUMMARY

- Nursing degree programmes vary in both content and length, lasting either three or four years.
- Entry requirements vary, but generally two or more GCE A levels at grade C or above are expected.
- Students applying for a first degree normally qualify for a mandatory grant from their local education authority.

6

CHOOSING A COURSE

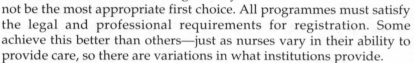

You may be surprised at
the variety of preregis-
tration programmes that are
available, although some will
have limited options—for school-
leavers without A levels, a degree may
not be the most appropriate first choice. All programmes must satisfy
the legal and professional requirements for registration. Some
achieve this better than others—just as nurses vary in their ability to
provide care, so there are variations in what institutions provide.

It is well worth taking the time to find out what students already
studying at a college or institute of higher education think of the programme (bearing in mind that some people are never pleased, no
matter how good the course!). A broad enquiry will make you aware
of the good and the not-so-good aspects of the course, and may pre-
vent you spending three or more years in an unsuitable environment. It could be argued that first impressions count, and that the
appearance of the site, and the demeanour, smiles and otherwise, of
the staff and students can say much. A drab educational environment with no evidence of care to enliven the surroundings does little
to enthuse either staff or students. A sense of liveliness, and evidence
of innovation and creativity, should provide students with stimula-
tion and help maintain enthusiasm across the board.

Remember, it's your choice to study in a place as much as it is
their choice to have you. You will be committing yourself to at least
three precious years of very hard work, so take every opportunity to
satisfy yourself that the place(s) to which you apply appeal to you. It
is often a good idea to contact the admissions tutors at the institu-
tion(s) which interest you, in order to arrange an informal visit. The
advantage of such a visit is that you have an opportunity to assess
the course and its philosophy and, equally importantly, the general
'feel' of the place. Another advantage is that you may be able to create a favourable first impression of yourself, always an asset prior to
an interview.

The choice of a Project 2000 programme versus a traditional course will soon disappear, leaving the options of either a degree or a diploma programme. If being a practical nurse appeals more than academic depth initially, then clearly the Project 2000 or non-degree route may be the most appropriate. However, if you thrive on academe as well as a desire to nurse, then a degree programme ought to stretch you, giving a good base from which to practise when qualified. All nurses have the opportunity to develop practical nursing skill. Claims that only traditional courses produce skilled practitioners are untrue, so don't be misled by some people's tales.

THE FUTURE
Graduates have a clear advantage in the long term—with job opportunities becoming fewer in number, employers may well restrict applications for more senior posts (e.g. sister or charge nurse) to graduates. Having said that, many Registered Nurses choose to delay studies for a degree until they have obtained some years of practical nursing experience. This option is increasingly favoured, with some taking degrees in speciality areas outside of, but appropriate to, nursing: for example, social and natural sciences. There are increasing opportunities for this route, so opting for a non-degree preregistration course need not be a final and irreversible decision.

Whatever your initial area of interest, time spent talking to others will be worthwhile, as will arranging to speak informally with staff at institutions to which you may wish to apply.

You may be surprised at the variety of courses available.

SUMMARY

- Nursing degree programmes generally occupy more of each year, as there is a need to ensure students receive enough clinical experience.
- Nursing degrees are much more intellectually demanding than other preregistration programmes.
- Graduates will generally fare better in the employment market, as nursing moves forward.
- Reading for a degree is in itself a significant developer of individuals, and provides for more awareness throughout life.
- Students are traditionally short of money, therefore lifestyles need to be tailored accordingly.

APPLYING FOR PLACES

FIRST IMPRESSIONS COUNT

As with many events in life, making an application for a place on a course involves human interaction. Such interactions inevitably lead to the creation of impressions concerning the applicant's suitability or otherwise for the post or course in question. In the case of interviews, there can be no doubt that the first impression leads to the formation of certain opinions about the candidate; these opinions may become fixed within the first few minutes, rendering subsequent interaction relatively unimportant. From this it may be assumed that first impressions count. You must create a favourable set of feelings and opinions about yourself in the eyes of those to whom you apply. Perhaps this is an appropriate time to consider what you would seek from an applicant were you the interviewer or admissions tutor.

Try the following exercise:
Make a list of your good Points. Be positive—you are a unique and valuable person. (Being positive does not mean being smug or self-important!)

-
-
-
-
-
-

Examine the list you have made—are there areas of overlap, or is each a discrete quality? How relevant and appropriate are these qualities to the course?

Now ask a friend to honestly list your good points.

-
-
-
-
-

Do the two lists match?

THE APPLICATION LETTER

If the letter is requesting application forms and further details it should contain the request only, and not reams of personal information. Your personal details will accompany the application form later. However, you will eventually have to write a letter of application. As with everything else:

- Keep it neat, and in your own handwriting.
- Do not waffle.
- Keep the contents concise but informative.
- Be positive.

Don't be afraid to identify weaknesses where appropriate:

I have experienced some difficulty in mathematics, but I have been undertaking extra study to remedy this, and my tutor feels that I should obtain grade A or B in the June examinations.

Such an admission demonstrates maturity, and will impress the reader.

THE APPLICATION FORM

You will have requested an application form from the Nurses and Midwives Central Clearing House (NMCCH) in the case of Project 2000 or traditional courses, or from The University or Polytechnic Central Admission Service (UCCA or PCAS—to be merged in 1994— see Appendix, *Useful Addresses*).

When you receive the application form, photocopy it and use the photocopy as a trial run—complete this in pencil and show it to someone else, taking note of their comments. *Never* complete an application form in ink right away.

Admissions tutors are not impressed by slapdash application forms. They receive many applications so yours must stand out as good, not sloppy.

It is not essential to complete the application using a typewriter, as neat handwriting is always impressive. Make sure that your writing is large enough to be clearly legible even if the form is reduced in size (e.g. for distribution to several institutions). If your application is difficult to read, busy admissions tutors may not take the time to decipher it.

WHAT SHOULD THE SUPPORTING LETTER CONTAIN?

The contents of the letter supporting your application should demonstrate insight into what it is that you are applying for, and the reasons why you are so interested. You should demonstrate that you are aware of the nature of both the subject and the (nursing) work that will follow it:

I have been interested in becoming a nurse since speaking to a friend's sister who is herself a nurse. I have also visited the library and read recent literature about nursing, as well as taking a nursing journal [specify which one] for the past six months.

The above demonstrates some insight into what may be involved in nursing, enough to want to pursue the subject. Compare it with the following:

I think I would like to work in a health-care area, perhaps nursing or occupational therapy or something similar.

If you don't know what you want, who does? Admissions tutors will not be impressed by this approach.

The letter should include your reasons for choosing the course, and why you are applying to that particular institution. You must therefore know what you want before you apply, for example by arranging an informal visit to talk with people who are involved in the areas in which you are interested. The notion of informal visits is an important one, in that it demonstrates a mature and sensible approach towards decision making. It also allows the prospective employer or tutor to make some assessment of you, and vice versa—a valuable asset when attending an interview.

Your letter should contain details of personal interests and achievements:

I have taken part in local community activities, making regular visits to an elderly lady, and helping out at a youth club, where I took charge of organising the spring fair. This involved fund-raising and publicity, as well as ensuring that there were adequate numbers of helpers. My hobbies include playing the flute, which I have studied to level 5, and I am a member of a local amateur dramatics group. I enjoy working with others, which is one of the reasons why nursing appeals...

37

Compare this to:

I sometimes go round to my friend's house at the weekend and listen to records.

This might be enjoyable, but is it really the sum total of your interests and achievements? However, do not succumb to the temptation to concoct an impressive-sounding list of interests and activities. An experienced interviewer will always find you out.

CURRICULUM VITAE (CV)
The CV is a list of your personal details and achievements in chronological order. It must accompany the application form and letter. A suggested format is given below.

CURRICULUM VITAE

NAME	Your surname followed by first names.
ADDRESS	Your home address and telephone number, or a contact number.
AGE	Your date and place of birth.
NEXT OF KIN	Name and relationship to you.
COURSE	The course or post for which you are applying.
EDUCATION	Give grades and dates, starting with your most recent educational experience. You should also include subjects studied but not passed; this will at least demonstrate that you have some knowledge of the subject. If you are presently studying then include details of the subjects, as this may be a useful point to bring out at interview.
WORK	Your work experience where appropriate, most recent first. Outline your main responsibilities.
HOBBIES	Brief details of your hobbies and interests.

THE INTERVIEW

Many colleges and universities will require you to attend an interview. This allows each party to assess the other's suitability. Remember, this is not a one-way test, nor are you on trial.

Attendance

When called for interview it is essential that you reply promptly, thanking them for their letter and confirming the date, time and place of the interview.

Be Early

Interviews are stressful for most people, and will be even more so if you have sprinted the last half-mile to the college, forgotten the envelope containing your qualifications, or neglected to check on times and reliability of public transport. So be early and arrive composed. If possible, take a few minutes to have a walk around.

Be early and arrive composed.

Appearance

Wear comfortable, tidy and, if possible, conventional clothing. You might like the latest fashions, but remember that first impressions are very important—you can show that you are an interesting person without looking off-puttingly voguish. Remember that every new student represents a considerable investment of time and money. The course interviewer has a responsibility to the college to see that the investment is wisely made, and will need reassurance that you can see beyond your immediate need for display.

The Interview Itself

There is usually more than one interviewer, each of whom is sure to ask at least one question:

- It is the quality of response that counts, so take time to think about what you are going to say.
- Speak clearly and evenly—a 'machine-gun' delivery, rattled off at great length and at top speed, will impress no-one.
- Avoid yes/no answers—explain your response.
- If you don't know the answer to a question, say so and offer an intelligent alternative. Similarly, if you don't understand a question, say so and ask for clarification. Interviewers are quick to criticise wafflers or those who fail to ensure that they understand what is being asked or discussed.
- Above all, be positive.

Practise these interview techniques with friends:

- Smile!—most interviewers like to see a smile.
- When shown to a chair sit comfortably—do not slouch.
- Avoid fidgeting, as this irritates everyone.
- Eye contact is crucial—share your eyes with the interviewers, and try to avoid favouring one and ignoring the others.

At the end of the interview you may be asked if you have any questions which you wish to put to the interviewers—do ask at least one question regarding the course for which you are applying. Think about this in advance of the interview, as it demonstrates insight and interest. At the end of the interview, ask when the college will let you know the decision.

The Decision

An Offer

Congratulations! Confirmation of the offer is usually sent in writing within a few weeks. Write back promptly if you are definitely going to take up the offer. NEVER accept and then fail to turn up, as your referees may be notified, and it could compromise you in the future. If you want a few days to consider the offer, say so, and then write back accepting (or rejecting). Better this than not turning up when arranged.

No Offer

Inevitably, there will be interviews which result in your not being offered a place. This is not something to take personally or to be seen as an irreversible failure. Be positive, and ask for feedback as to how you might strengthen future applications. You have a right to this feedback, which might turn out to be crucial to your future success.

MULTIPLE APPLICATIONS

You may wish to apply to more than one institution—this is not unusual and no-one is likely to be perturbed by your doing so. If they ask at the interview, you should tell them what other offers/interviews you have, and what your intentions are, e.g. you will accept this place if it is offered, or that you wish to follow up your other applications.

WHERE TO APPLY FOR COURSES

Colleges of nursing and institutions of higher education have their own central application system (NMCCH, and PCAS or UCCA). For information and application details, write direct to the appropriate service. (See Appendix, *Useful Addresses*.)

PROJECT 2000 AND TRADITIONAL PROGRAMS

This information applies only to full-time courses. If you are considering a part-time course, contact the appropriate university direct.

Applications are made through NMCCH and follow a timetable. Candidates apply to a maximum of four colleges offering nurse education programmes. Each institution considers the applications at the same time. The precise dates for each stage of the application process are announced each year, but the timing is broadly as follows.

Mid-September to Mid-December

An Applicant's Handbook is available from NMCCH. Applications are returned to NMCCH, and forwarded to colleges of health/nursing for short-listing.

Early January to Mid-May

Institutions interview short-listed candidates and notify NMCCH of their decisions. NMCCH then send offers of a place to study direct to the candidates, who must reply within fourteen days. The candidates' decisions (to accept or reject the offer of a place) are sent by NMCCH to the appropriate colleges.

If you are offered a place you have three options:

- Firmly accept the offer—other institutions will be informed of your decision and will cease to consider your application. Once you have firmly accepted an offer, you may not change your mind.
- Reject the offer—again, once you have firmly rejected an offer, you may not change your mind.
- Provisionally accept. This is useful if you are waiting for a decision from another institution. Only one such offer may be held. If you receive a second offer, then you have the right to firmly accept just one of them.

Mid-May to Early June
Remaining decisions are relayed to applicants, and responses are duly forwarded to appropriate colleges.

Early June to Mid-June
Final and outstanding candidates' decisions are sent to the relevant colleges.

Mid-June to Early September
The clearing system sends vacancy lists to candidates who have not yet obtained a place to study. It is each candidates' responsibility to contact the institutions concerned. The colleges hold further interviews and notify candidates of their decisions.

Early September to Late September
Unsuccessful candidates are referred for advice, and new application forms are dispatched. There is no extra charge for processing in the next fixed application period, although a new Applicant's Handbook must be paid for.

UNDERGRADUATE (DEGREE) PROGRAMS
The following information applies only to full-time courses. If you are considering a part-time course, contact the appropriate university direct.

Applications are made through PCAS (for universities recently created from polytechnics) or UCCA (for all other universities). UCCA and PCAS are to merge in 1994.

There is a deadline by which time all applications must be received, if they are to be considered. This deadline is normally sometime in mid-December of the year before the course is due to begin. Given the demand for places, it is advisable to send your application to your referee as early as possible, to enable him or her to complete your reference and get it into the system in good time. Should your application be received after cut-off date, you may be considered as a 'late applicant'. This cannot be relied upon, for example where courses have been filled.

OFFERS
There are three possible outcomes from your application:

1. An unconditional offer—you are guaranteed a place provided you accept.
2. A conditional offer—you need to satisfy certain conditions, i.e. obtain particular grades in exams.
3. Rejection—no offer is made.

Applicants who receive a postal rejection have no automatic right to discuss it with the institution concerned. However, if you are advised that you will not be offered a place at the end of the interview, you can ask for feedback as to how you could strengthen future applications.

WHAT TO DO WHEN OFFERED A PLACE

You must formally accept or reject the offer. If you do neither, then you may be rejected by default after a deadline has passed. Your acceptance of an offer can be one of the following:

• Firm—if the offer was unconditional, i.e. this is your first-choice institution. If you make a firm acceptance then you are bound to take up the place, and may be released only with the permission of the institution which holds the place for you.
• Conditional firm—if the offer is conditional.
• Conditional insurance—you will accept the offer of the place if you don't get your first choice. This is literally an insurance policy against not having a place to study.

CLEARING

Those who do not secure a firm offer of a place have the option of going through the clearing system. The application goes into a pool and is circulated amongst institutions who have vacancies. You are not obliged to accept places elsewhere, but this might be a more suitable option for some people than nowhere at all.

DEFERRED ENTRY

You may apply for a place, but to begin in a subsequent year, if for example you wish to take a year out before beginning your studies. The application process is as described above.

SUMMARY

• First impressions count. Be impressive.
• Know where you are and where you wish to go. Do your homework.
• Be neat, positive and clear in your application letter.
• Work on your CV, make it clear and well organised.
• Be early for interviews, don't panic—smile!
• Be positive—you are a unique and valuable person.
• You are bound to receive some rejections—learn from them!

MATURE
STUDENTS

INTRODUCTION

The term 'mature student' conjures up a certain image, a stereotype even—someone over the age of forty-five, who is fed up with his or her present career, or who has survived bringing up small children and now wishes to return to study. Such mature students can indeed be found. However, in the eyes of the higher education establishment you are 'mature' if you are over the age of twenty-one at entry.

The concept of mature student status has been around for many years, and the number of mature candidates applying for places on courses in general, and nursing courses in particular, rises every year. It is not uncommon for an institution of higher education to have up to half the students (across a variety of courses) falling into the mature category. This should come as no surprise, considering the increasing uncertainty of some occupations, combined with the nursing profession's ever-present need for carers who are both mature in outlook and knowledgeable .

The Benefits of Being a Mature Student

Although the decision to become a mature student involves certain risks, there are also benefits which more than compensate. Some people may have had little opportunity at school to realise their full potential, for social, economic, personal or other reasons. Returning to education gives them the opportunity to pursue a career which they might previously have thought to be beyond their reach, due to their lack of formal qualifications.

There may in some individuals be a 'reawakening'—in academic terms, the notion of late development. Whether this late development is due to some rising of latent cognitive abilities, or is simply the realisation that learning did not stop irrevocably upon leaving school, varies between individuals.

This chapter briefly examines some of the issues confronting the mature candidate.

ENTRANCE REQUIREMENTS

The general entry requirements for diploma and degree courses have been discussed elsewhere (see Chapters 3, 4 and 5). In the case of mature candidates, consideration may be given for work, life experience and so on; this is known as Accreditation of Prior Experiential Learning (APEL). (For this reason, it is always useful to compile a portfolio of achievements, as it is an impressive addition to any application.)

Although the APEL may well make up for a lack of formal academic qualifications, mature candidates who fulfil the institution's standard requirements do have an advantage over those without qualifications or evidence of recent study. In fact, it is probably unwise to attempt a course of study for nursing without recent experience of some form of academic work. All courses make certain intellectual demands, but academically inexperienced students face additional difficulties on returning to the discipline of study. For example, many students find the natural sciences taught at the beginning of a nursing course more difficult to learn than the humanities (which may be said to have roots in life experience and to be more open to debate and interpretation). A student who has not recently studied sciences up to GCE A level or equivalent may well find that these problems are multiplied.

These difficulties can certainly be eased by a programme of preparation, for example by attending evening classes in appropriate topics. Consult someone who actually teaches nursing—he or she will be able to identify which subjects will give most benefit when the course actually begins. (This kind of preparation is sure to impress the selectors.) Although institutions generally welcome non-standard applications from mature people, there are definite advantages in being able to provide evidence of appropriate, recent study.

FINANCIAL CONSIDERATIONS

Money (or the lack of it) is a major consideration for most applicants to nursing courses, and there can be no doubt that short-term sacrifices do have to be made. Many students have difficulty managing on their grants or bursaries alone, although a mature student may be able to obtain some kind of part-time work, particularly where he or she possesses a saleable skill.

Mature students are generally able to claim allowances over and above the local authority grants, especially if they have dependents. However, once a spouse's income passes a certain level, the position can be reversed—she or he must pay part of the (meagre) grant award, thus further reducing the household's income. Precise details of your own grant entitlement for a first degree should be sought from your local education authority offices.

Bursaries (awarded for Project 2000 courses) are generally non-means tested. A student on this type of programme is likely to be financially better off if, for example, the spouse has a reasonable income and would otherwise have had to contribute.

Students are often highly regarded by bank managers, in view of their potential as wage earners, and so may be able to secure loans relatively easily. Tread very carefully here, as many students relying on loans get deeply into debt and find themselves having to work long hours, often at the expense of coursework and risk of failure, in order to pay back their loans. A more sensible solution might be to build up some financial reserves before embarking on a course.

THE STUDENT ROLE

Re-entering the field of study, the majority of your peers will probably be under 21 years of age. For most mature students the process of integration does not cause undue problems, and for many, acceptance by a group of younger students is a rewarding and fulfilling second bite at the cherry of youth. Regardless of the age gap, there will exist the common bond of subject interest. The life experience of a mature group member may enable her to offer a perspective on certain issues which, if presented in a non-patronising way, may well be accepted and fruitful.

Some colleges and universities arrange discussion groups for mature students, in which common interests can be shared and where mutual support can be found. Even where there is no formal arrangement, mature students will establish links with each other.

Teachers enjoy teaching mature students, as they usually demonstrate palpable motivation, and a real interest in the subject. In younger students this kind of application, although present, competes with other demands of youth and new-found freedom.

CHANGING STATUS

As you adopt (consciously or not) the role of student, the change in status will make some adjustments necessary. Some have to deal with uncomprehending or even hostile reactions from friends and family. Janet is a female student in her 30s, married with children:

My cultural background didn't support women going to study. [My family and friends] thought I was a bit odd, couldn't work out why I wanted to do [the course]. Some even tried to put me off. Overall my parents were supportive, but my husband just didn't want to know. I have a friend who is also a mature student. We support each other—she's not a nurse, but we share experiences. Coming back to study has opened my eyes. I think I'm moving away from my culture. I'm more aware now, more self confident, I know what I want.

I wasn't sure what college would be like, thought that because of my age I'd feel like a fish out of water, but also that I'd find lectures easier. I found that I was able to deal with problems better—I've had more experience of life, and having kids has helped me appreciate the needs of others. I find I get on well with other students. They treat me the same as anyone else, although they sometimes ask me for advice.... I used to feel guilty that I wasn't getting things done at home, that the house had to wait. I don't feel so bad about it now—I'm getting used to it!

I don't know what made me want to study nursing. I went to FE college and really enjoyed that—it showed me how different adult learning is to the dogmas of school. I'm glad I took A levels, I'd strongly recommend that. When I've finished this course, I want to get about a year's experience as a staff nurse, then hopefully take on some more study—I've got a taste for it now. I would say to anyone thinking about being a mature student, go for it!

Some people believe that we get but one attempt at education, and that to return to study is a sure sign that one is 'a bit odd' if not downright bohemian. Bear with it—it is for most a rewarding experience, one which almost all admit to being grateful for.

ORGANISING YOUR HOME LIFE

Help with household chores is a must. Things that you and your family used to take for granted will become irritating 'extra' jobs to be done. Rather than argue each day about who does what, give out lists of regular jobs, and rotate the most hated tasks. That way fairness is ensured and people know what is expected of them. Stick to the rota, and be consistent. Give special treats to eager participants—a day off, a trip to the cinema, or just a big hug. Share these yourself: you deserve them, too. Make your loved ones feel extra special, show them that you really appreciate them and that you couldn't manage without their help—they will feel they have a share in your success. You are going to be less available during the course, so make the time that you have together really count. Don't just sit around feeling bored, or catching up on routine chores—go out, meet friends or get friends to come round and make them feel part of your endeavour, too. Talk about your course by all means, but remember that what you find so interesting may seem dull to the uninitiated.

Spouses or partners, children and close friends can all feel left out of your life. These people are vital to you, so keep interested in them. You will stand a better chance of survival and at the same time get a much-needed break from thinking about the course.

Make sure that you have somewhere to study and work away from the hustle and bustle of the family. If you don't have some kind of study room, clear a corner somewhere where you can sit reasonably quietly to work. Study usually involves sitting for long periods, so a firm, comfortable cushion is a must.

SUMMARY

- The challenge of a course of study as a mature student is, if prepared for and properly thought out, undeniably rewarding.

- Obstacles such as low income and the rearrangement of domestic circumstances are surmountable, but you may have to make some sacrifices, and will rely heavily on friends and family.

- Close friends and family will notice the change in you. In some cases gaps will form in existing relationships. A person who was interesting before your course might be less so once your mind has been sharpened. A profound statement but true.

- Organise yourself and family. Make time for them.

A final word to those still unsure of their potential to succeed. For whatever reason, be it peer group pressure, social and domestic circumstances or even the pains of adolescence, some people simply aren't able to realise their full study potential when at school. Seek to improve your confidence through a recognition of past achievements. Think hard about what you would really like to get out of the proposed course of study—with the right encouragement and support you have as good a chance as most others of success in your chosen field.

GO FOR IT!

9

SURVIVAL AWAY FROM HOME

The majority of nursing students are school-leavers who have spent most of their lives in the comfort of the family home. Leaving this safety to go out into the world is for most a daunting experience, tinged with the excitement and anticipation of new-found freedom and the chance to be really independent for the first time. Very few would consider the experience in a negative light, many viewing its maturing influence as an essential stage in their newly acquired adulthood. You too will change, hopefully for the better.

There are an almost infinite number and variety of obstacles to be overcome, some more pleasurable than others. The feelings you encounter will range from panic, terror, loneliness and frustration, to the exhilaration of freedom, the joys of developing new friendships and skills, and an appreciation of a new environment.

Emma, Katy, Alice and Jenny are all third-year nursing students. Their cultural and regional backgrounds are as diverse as their expectations.

Emma I think being away from home lived up to my expectations—college is a little how I imagined public school would be, but more lenient... I was in the halls of residence, which gave freedom of who to socialise with. There are disadvantages, for example when you move into a shared house... you have to do the washing and cooking, make sure there's enough toilet paper, and so on... that's when you realise there's so much more to do... but the freedom's great, you can eat what and when you like, if you fancy curry for breakfast (which I sometimes do) then that's OK.

Alice I was looking forward to it, but when I found how hard it was to get a house I was really scared... When I did finally get a house it was awful at first, we just didn't get on... there was conflict... there were age differences and one of the girls smoked which bothered me a lot coming from a non-smoking background, although later we got on fine.

Emma Even in the halls of residence there was still friction, sometimes you just didn't dare go out.

Emma and Alice Living in an all-girl house there can a lot of bitchiness and competition. It can be hard to get some people to help with the housework, so you end up doing it yourself... also where there are too many nurses in the same house it can be boring, as all people talk about is nursing.

Jenny I found myself feeling very homesick and lonely when others in the house went home at weekends... I was left on my own and they were able to go home. I know one girl, who cried herself to sleep the first two weeks— sometimes others would be supportive but not always. I knew a girl, an only child, who phoned home all the time and who went home every weekend... it seems to defeat the object really, leaving to study away from home but being back home every week.

Katy I found a big problem in racism, one of the girls in the house was very prejudiced, she kept asking me if I understood Japanese when I don't come from anywhere near Japan... she has left now thank goodness.

Emma I think a mixed house is best, where there are blokes. They behave well and are really helpful... they don't try to be all macho... people find it easier to visit the house where there's a mix of people, they feel less intimidated.

Katy Another thing that no-one tells you about is landlords—they can be really difficult, especially when you want something done... even the affiliated student union housing can be awkward... it isn't always what you expect.

Emma When you are feeling low, it would be nice to feel there was someone there to turn to for help. There is support from the staff, but it feels a bit formal. Most of the time I thought it was fun being here, although I had been away from home before... I enjoyed the parties and freshers' nights... great fun.

Alice I think it's really worthwhile moving away from home... I find myself being much more confident now.

All Advice to give to new students... visit the city first to get a feel for the place, make sure you get to know who the good landlords are and which areas are best to look for a house—better still, try to get into halls of residence to begin with, so you can get to know people and look round for a place to live... it would be worth setting up contacts with students who have been on the course for a while so you can get to know a bit more about the course and the city... Taking a year out to travel before starting the course would be worthwhile, it helps you get to know yourself better and to get the feel of being away from home—if you can get a job the money always helps.

BEATING THE BLUES

Many students identify similar difficulties in their early days in a strange environment, away from home. It is important to get to know other people, not necessarily students, although they are likely to be most accessible to you. Join a society or club; most hospitals and colleges have some, and all universities have many. You will meet people there who share a common interest and a desire to do something constructive with their spare time. As you recognise familiar faces you will begin to feel as if you belong somewhere, which should help you to settle.

Never sit alone in your room feeling sorry for yourself—misery loves its own company, and will thrive in making you feel dreadful. Don't be afraid to admit that you feel lonely or homesick—getting it into the open often helps to blow some of the feeling away. Interestingly enough, there are often others who are as lonely as you sometimes feel and who, like you, may not think anyone else could feel that way. It is all too easy only to see those who are constantly out enjoying themselves.

Go For Balance

Burning the candle at both ends is often driven by a fear of failure, but comes with a high price. If you had all the skills and knowledge to be a nurse, then you wouldn't need to be on the course. However, you are unlikely to get the most out of the course if your eyelids are propped open by matchsticks, due to several very late nights and an inadequate balance of diet, rest and exercise. Take a look at what you eat—is it quick snacks on the run, or a healthy balance of nourishing food needed for a healthy brain and body? Go for walks or try to take some form of enjoyable exercise, and remember that over-worked, overtired and miserable is a recipe for disaster.

Organise your life

Organised students are more successful than brilliant but disorganised ones, so make plans. Get a large pad of writing paper and leave it in a place where you can always find it easily. Use the pad for making out a weekly list of jobs to do. Prioritise these into 'A', 'B' and 'C' categories. Throw away the 'C's, as they aren't worth bothering with. Look carefully at the 'A's and 'B's. Give the 'A's priority, and leave yourself a reasonable amount of time to complete them.

Above all, don't allow yourself to get sidetracked! We can all think of ten things we'd rather do when there is something we don't particularly want to do. We can all sit around with a head full of ideas about all the tasks building up and up, until they wear us down and down. Forget it! Time is too precious. Get on with the 'A' tasks and, if there's time, do a few 'B's, but don't just sit there!

Get Out!
Don't forget that you need lots of exercise in order to keep brain and body in shape.

Talk to Other Students
It may sound crazy, but you'll learn as much from your classmates as from your tutors, if not more. Compare your understanding of the morning's lecture with theirs, throw a few ideas around about the topic, share information with each other.

Consider Not Phoning Home More Than Once Every Fortnight
If you're feeling low then a phone call home will really drag you through the floor. Write a letter home instead. Make a list of three positive things that happened recently, tell them what the weather's like, what so-and-so said in class yesterday, and so on. Your friends and family will want to read these thoughts, so share them, and be positive.

If things are really bad and you feel like crying, go ahead, and then put on some music and tidy up your room—or better still, go round and help someone else tidy theirs.

SUMMARY
- Take care of yourself—eat properly and take time out to do what you want to do.
- Don't study all the time.
- Avoid people who constantly criticise, moan or whinge; they will tire you and colour your moods.
- Hobbies are vital—develop an existing one, or find a new one and with it new friends.
- Exercise regularly, preferably with others.
- Make friends with non-nurses and broaden your circle of friends.
- Take each day as it comes.
- Always try to see the positive side, even if this seems impossible.
- Set realistic goals for yourself.
- Manage your time, both at work and at play.
- Manage your money, although it may be scarce.
- Take a course in managing stress.
- Maintain a sense of humour.
- Make haste slowly.

10

STUDY SKILLS

Most people starting a nursing course have already sat exams and completed study assignments, and probably feel that they have reasonable study skills. This may be true for a few people; it is certainly not true of most.

Study, like survival away from home, requires planning and consistency if success is to be more than just a twist of fate. A balance of study and leisure is essential. We all know people who prefer to 'cram' the night before an assignment is due, or even the night before exams. This is a foolish misdirection of mental and physical energy. Cramming might exercise your intellect for a short period, but whether any real understanding or learning takes place is debatable.

GO FOR A PLAN OF STUDY

Many people find that they cannot study effectively for more than forty minutes at a time. Burning the midnight oil really only benefits the manufacturers of light bulbs (or oil lamps), so back off. Spend forty minutes on concentrated study or revision, then go for a walk, stretch, listen to ten minutes of music, or simply close your eyes and think of something, somewhere or someone pleasant. Then go back for another forty minutes. This way you will have the mental space to understand more of what you are studying. As a result you will learn more, creating a firm foundation on which to build your knowledge and maximise your chances of success. Remember, you will work better if you make creative use of your leisure time.

AVOIDING PROBLEMS

If you find that you are staring at the words on the page but nothing is sinking in, STOP! There is something in the queue for your attention. It could be a problem or some other issue which you haven't yet sorted out. Go for a short walk and let your mind wander. Let your thoughts come and go until one thought sticks—this could be the culprit. Think it through, have a warm drink, then return to your study with what should be a clearer mind. If things are no better, write the study topic in your 'To do' pad, and give it priority 'A'. Forget the study for now, as you will simply become frustrated, but don't use this as an excuse to avoid it later.

BUYING BOOKS

Most courses come with a list of recommended books. Don't try to buy them all; instead, go to the lecturer who made the recommendation and ask for an outline of the main areas addressed by each book. This will help you to decide which books you really need to buy, and which you could take out from the library. Some students find it useful to buy several different books between them as a shared reference. If you choose to do this it will prove a great time- and money-saver. Make sure, however, that you keep a list of who owns what, and a note of who has each book at any one time—this will help to avoid disputes later.

Before you buy a book, scan the pages to get some idea of the prose style—is it written in a laborious style guaranteed to send you to sleep, or is the author able to maintain your interest? Also check to see if it covers the topic areas which you need to study.

JOURNAL ARTICLES

Most lecturers/tutors recommend that you read journal articles. They are usually more up-to-date than books, and are a very useful source of reference. However, you shouldn't waste time photocopying an article unless you really need it word for word: you will need to take it away with you to work on later, which makes it into yet another chore, or you will just file it away never to be seen again.

> What I hear, I forget
> What I see, I remember
> What I do, I understand.
> (Chinese proverb)

Be involved in doing something with the article. Don't copy it out word for word—make your own notes on what the author is saying. Paraphrasing the article will give you some personal investment in it, and will make it easier to remember the details. When you have finished, make a careful note of the journal's title and date, and the title and page number of the article. There can be few things so frustrating as thumbing through your notes for information, finding exactly what you are looking for, but not knowing where it came from.

After spending time with the article, go away and pamper yourself for being so organised!

LECTURES

We've all seen people who frantically write down everything that the lecturer says, word for word. This is a waste of time. For learning to take place there must be understanding—all the avid note-taker does is to transcribe what is said directly onto the page, so the ideas bypass the brain.

Be part of the lecture. The most important thing is to listen to what is said. Write down key words or phrases, and any reference material suggested by the speaker. This way you are involved in what is happening, and not simply a spectator (see Chinese proverb, above).

After the lecture, go and ask the speaker for references if none were offered. If something is unclear, ask a question, either straight away or at the end. Tutors love to expand on what they are teaching, so don't be embarrassed—there are probably other students who also didn't understand and who are, like you, afraid to ask.

ESSAY WRITING

This one really throws a lot of people, when a few simple rules may make all the difference.

Let us first consider why anyone would want you to write an essay:

- To demonstrate your understanding of a topic.
- To demonstrate your ability to express your thoughts and write clearly.
- To demonstrate your ability to analyse issues through discussion.
- To get you to organise your thinking.
- To allow tutors to find out where you might need help for further development.

Planning Your Essay

Like anything else to do with effective study, essays must be planned. In fact, it is unlikely that anyone would start to build anything without planning first. Imagine a builder deciding where to put the next room in a new house only when he had finished building the last one. The result could be a series of unconnected boxes, with the builder stuck behind the garage, without the space to get out. Essays can turn out a bit like that, so make sure you have a plan. Before you begin, try this checklist:

- What is the main question, or are there several?
- What is the suggested number of words?
- Where can I gather the information I need?
- How long have I been allowed?

Brainstorming

Brainstorming is the spontaneous jotting down of words, ideas and phrases which immediately come to mind about a topic. Allow yourself about two minutes to brainstorm some ideas for inclusion in your essay. Here is an example for an essay on kangaroos (about which I know very little).

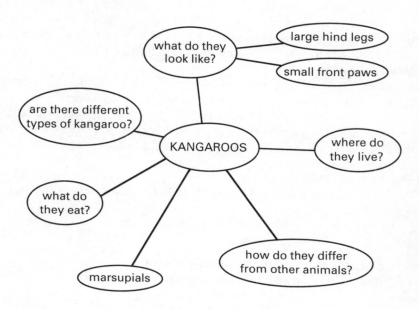

Sort your ideas into categories, and plan where each idea will go in the essay. For example, it seems logical that the kangaroo's appearance and habitat should come before a description of its food or mating habits.

In essays as with examinations, it is vital that you read the question very carefully and underline the main points. Does the essay ask for a particular focus? For example: *Discuss the effect of urbanisation on the red kangaroo.* This essay asks for focus, through historical and social development, on a particular species of kangaroo. Issues of urbanisation—what does it mean, why has it come about—need to be included in your plan. Although it is useful to identify traits of kangaroos in general, the red kangaroo is the focus, and its particular attributes will need to be brought out in the essay. (Don't worry, kangaroo theory is not part of the nursing curriculum.)

Once the essay is planned then it can be written. This should be the easy bit—you will have all the necessary details in front of you, and a plan of what goes where, so drafting the essay should be relatively straightforward.

An Essay Is Like A Hot-Air Balloon

What, I hear you ask, has a hot-air balloon in common with an essay? Well, let's take a look. An essay should have three parts:

• An introduction—the main points are briefly identified.
• The main text—about 80% of the total essay, where the main points are discussed in detail.
• The conclusion—a very important section, in which the main points are summarised and the arguments are tied together.

But what about the balloon ?
Consider the diagram below:

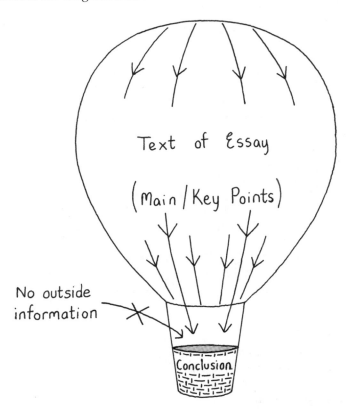

• The balloon is the main body of text.
• The basket underneath is the conclusion, where all the strings (main points) come together. Remember that at this point nothing new may be brought in from outside.
• The introduction describes the whole, just as an observer might describe the hot-air balloon flying past their window to someone unfamiliar with balloons.

ASSESSMENTS

There are two main types of assessment.

Summative assessments count towards your final grade. Examples are driving tests and examinations. Formative assessments are designed to give you feedback on your progress, and are not included in the calculation of your final grade. Examples are 'dummy run' driving tests and mock examinations.

Most courses include a variety of assessments, including project work, individual and group work and, horror of horrors... exams.

SUCCESS IN EXAMINATIONS

Preparation

It should come as no surprise to learn that the key to examination success is... planning!

Prepare well in advance of the exam, following the advice on how to study (see above). There should no need to burn the midnight oil the evening before the exam. Instead, go for a walk to clear your head and get some oxygen to the vital areas. The walk might also help you get a good night's sleep, leaving you with a clear head.

If the exam is in the morning, allow enough time for an unhurried breakfast. Don't drink lots of tea or coffee—this will make you more likely to need the toilet during the exam, wasting valuable time. If the exam is in the afternoon, have a light, easily digestible lunch, such as a sandwich. If you have a heavy meal you will be too sleepy to concentrate. In short, eat sensibly!

Get there early, don't rush in at the last minute. Ensure that you have spare pens, chewing gum etc. Do not listen to the last-minute panics of friends, or their (usually incorrect) information on the topic to be examined, as this will throw you into confusion. If you have planned properly, you should be ready for anything.

The Exam

Selecting Questions

Always read all the questions before writing anything. What appears to be an ideal question may turn out to be a nightmare. Once you have decided which questions you are going to answer, you can begin to plan your writing.

Planning the Essays

Read through each question again, and underline the main issues. Don't write anything yet! This might seem worrying to you initially, but there is a powerful reason behind this approach.

Now is the time to brainstorm ideas for every question that you plan to answer. By the time you have brainstormed ideas for the second or third question you will probably remember something else to include in the first. If you want to prove that this works, just think back to your experience of writing essays—have you ever got towards the end of the essay and suddenly remembered something which you ought to have included, but haven't ? Your mind sometimes needs a little extra time to process information—not everything comes to mind immediately. If further proof is needed, think back to the last time you had a discussion (or argument) with a friend—when he or she left, you almost certainly remembered something you should have said (or wish you had said). Convinced ?

Brainstorming ideas for all the questions gets a lot of the thinking out of the way in the first few minutes of the exam, while your mind is still fresh. You can now begin to put together your answers, as suggested in the earlier section on essay writing. Leave the rough work for the examiner to see, as it may demonstrate that you have a wider understanding of the topic than you were able to include in your answer.

Exam Technique (Don't Panic!)

The next piece of advice is likely to meet with some resistance, but it really does work. In an exam, as when studying, there is a limit to how long anyone can perform without a short break. You may well be able to write for two or three hours, but not with any quality—you need a break, so *rest your brain*. During the exam you should put your pen down every hour for one or two minutes and close your eyes. Do not panic, as this really works in your favour. Your mind will be refreshed and you will continue with renewed mental energy. Indeed, if you spend a few minutes resting each hour during the exam, you will almost certainly find that you have more than that amount of time left at the end of the exam.

After the Exam

Never have an exam post mortem immediately afterwards. This is bound to dispirit you and has no value. Instead, go for a coffee or a short walk. Don't try studying the same day or evening for another exam, as your mind will keep going back to the one you've just completed, hampering your concentration.

Remember, organisation is the key to success!

SUMMARY

- Study with friends—you will learn from each other.
- Join or start a support group, and share problems.
- Study in measured amounts, not all the time.
- Don't panic—study methodically, not in a hurry.
- Take time out for rest between study periods.
- Be positive.
- Take one thing at a time.
- Set realistic goals.
- Read, read, read anything—articles, books, lecture notes.
- Be organised; develop a system of filing notes.
- Plan your week as far as possible.
- Attend lectures, as the lecturer will have study material that would take you many hours to prepare.
- Photocopy only when unavoidable—make notes on the spot instead.
- Do 'it' today, for tomorrow something else will need doing.
- Don't take on more than you can handle.
- Eat, exercise and play appropriately.
- Remember, teachers are human too, they have all been there and done that, and they too have to work hard, so be nice to them.

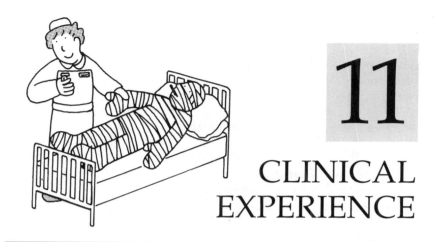

11

CLINICAL EXPERIENCE

Those who choose nursing do so because they wish to work with people. All nursing students are eager to get out of the classroom and into clinical areas, to get some 'hands on' experience and feel like a 'real' nurse. Clinical experience will vary according to the area, and the people with whom you find yourself working. This experience can be interesting, enjoyable, or distressing—indeed, all of your emotions (and muscles) will be exercised through clinical work.

THE PLACEMENT

Before you are due to begin your clinical placement, contact the nurse in charge and introduce yourself. Ask if there is anything particular about their clinical area which you should know about, or anything you ought to do before you start.

Try to arrive at least ten minutes early. This will allow you to begin composed, and may give you the opportunity to talk to other staff while they are free of the demands of the care area. Always be smart and tidy when in clinical, as you will score no points for looking like last month's washing. (Needless to say, you can look how you wish away from clinical.)

Get On With Your Colleagues

The extent to which you enjoy your work will be tailored by you—if you are constantly late, untidy, rude and demanding, then busy nurses will give you short shrift.

You must make the effort to get on with staff. They will colour your enjoyment of the placement, and will certainly prefer to work with you and support you if you are friendly, cheerful and sensible.

Be Assertive

Leave personal problems at home, and certainly don't take your moods out on staff in clinical areas. However, there may be times when you are unhappy about the way in which you or others are being treated. If this is the case, be assertive (not belligerent), and discuss the problem with the person involved. If this brings no joy, ask to speak to whoever is in charge at the time. If you still feel aggrieved, seek support from your tutor. Most difficulties are easily resolved by adult-to-adult negotiation. Simply being assertive does not mean that you will be labelled as a troublemaker.

You are in clinical placement to learn, so don't allow yourself to be used only for menial, repetitious and educationally worthless tasks. Everyone from the ward sister down has to do these jobs sometimes, but no student or qualified nurse should be doing them all the time. The key question to ask yourself is: "Am I being asked to do something that is educationally beneficial, or am I just being used as cheap labour?"

Smile!

People respond to smilers, even if only to ask what you're smiling about. Patients definitely like to see someone who is caring for them smile; it conveys something of your desire to be there with them.

STRESS MANAGEMENT

When you look after people you give something of yourself, and this emotional commitment is bound to have an effect—many experienced nurses clearly remember stressful experiences going back years. However, you must try not to take your clinical work home with you. It is no good for you or for anyone else if you find that you cannot let go of the stress and worry which almost inevitably accompanies some clinical experience.

Talk to someone about what is bothering you. All nurses will have some empathy with what you are feeling, so find a soulmate and unload some of your fears or concerns. A trouble shared really is a trouble halved, and she or he might need the favour returned sometime.

Given the demanding nature of many clinical placements, it is important that you ensure adequate recreation as a counterbalance. You may feel that there just isn't enough time in the week for leisure, especially if you are working shifts, but make the effort. You need your recreation, now more than ever before. Adequate rest, recreation and diet are essential.

Nurses seem to gravitate together in social situations, and when they do they talk about—that's right—nursing. Try to find at least one friend who is not a nurse. This oasis will be valuable to you as a respite from your working life.

Some people will advise you never to get involved with your patients. Well, you would have to be made of stone to be able to do this all of the time. Getting involved is part of nursing, and you do not become 'hardened' as the years pass. Many very experienced clinical nurses still shed a tear occasionally, although Western culture seems to find this difficult to understand. After all, we are human beings! You will learn to develop coping strategies as an essential means of survival. One of these is, as mentioned earlier, sharing your concerns with others.

IT'S NOT ALL (DIS)STRESS

The vast majority of nurses stay in clinical practice. The reasons for this include the fact that the work can be extremely satisfying and rewarding. It may be argued that nowhere is there work which offers so much on a personal level, including variety, opportunities for creativity and the sense of belonging to a team. The media inform us that people are enjoying better health now than ever before, and this is thanks to the progress in health care of which nurses are a part. Being able to share quality-of-life decisions with patients gives the nurse enormous satisfaction. Multiply this by the number of people for whom you may care each day, and you multiply the satisfactions. This is not meant to paint a misleadingly rosy picture (the opposite can be true), but most nurses will agree that the positive aspects— satisfaction and a sense of personal fulfilment—are very real.

SUMMARY

- Work at getting on with others.
- Learn how to manage stress.
- Don't take your personal problems into clinical, and don't take your clinical problems home.
- Share your concerns with staff, friends, family, tutors.
- Enjoy the rewards of clinical work.
- Make every effort to ensure adequate rest, exercise and a balanced diet.

12

THE NEWLY REGISTERED NURSE

FACTS OF LIFE

So the course is completed and the security of college life is behind you. The wider world beckons and the prospect of being able to put your qualification after your name can only add to what must be a sense of elation and self-satisfaction, tinged, no doubt, with a little apprehension.

The years of study are likened by some to the gradual filling of a vessel which when full (on qualifying) contains everything necessary to practise as a nurse. This is a misconception. Most newly qualified nurses very quickly realise that they have a 'knowledge deficit', that despite their years of study they simply don't have all the answers. The simple truth is that neither you, nor anyone else, will ever have all the answers. The main purpose of your education is to hone your analytical skills, to enable you to think problems through and find a solution. Of course, you will also have learnt some hard facts, but many more will follow as you integrate what you have learnt into new situations.

CHOICE OF JOBS

In nursing, as with many other occupations, there are times when jobs are plentiful, and times when they are not. Either way, you will be eager to begin work, and should choose carefully where to start. If you have no burning ambition to work in any particular area, then a period of 6–12 months learning the role of staff nurse will be time well spent. For many newly qualified nurses, this usually means a post as staff nurse in a hospital ward. Some will return to a ward which they worked in as a student, because they had a particularly good experience there, or because they found the work interesting. Others would never dream of doing this, possibly because they found the staff unsympathetic, or because the work in that area just didn't appeal to them.

Try to get a balance of experience in the early years, as too specialised a background might make it difficult for you to transfer into other areas later on. For example, if you have already spent 6–12 months in a non-acute area, a further 6–12 months in an acute area would allow you to consolidate and widen your experience. This is by no means a rigid formula. Ask other, more experienced staff nurses for their advice.

Take care not to fall into the trap of having too narrow a range of experience. This tends to promote a blinkered view of the wider world of nursing, and more often than not leads to very rigid views about the business of nursing. This can be detrimental both for the nurse and for the patients. A broad spread of nursing experience in the first two years will give you a firm foundation on which to base your career development.

OVERHEARD AT COFFEE-TIME
The following comments were gleaned from the conversation of a group of newly qualified nurses working in a variety of clinical speciality areas.

Their Concerns...
I feel nervous when I'm talking to students, they seem to expect you to know all the answers.... Being left in charge early on is a worry, especially if you don't get much support. You feel that you don't have the managerial skills to delegate... especially when the other nurses are more experienced than you and you have to delegate jobs to them—you feel as if they don't have confidence in you because of your lack of experience.... the responsibility can be frightening... it's also hard when you feel you have to go against what the doctors are wanting.... I've seen some really bad practice, and I hate trying to stand up against it—some nurses' practices are so ritualistic, it's hard to get them to stop and look at what they're doing... I'm afraid of letting other people down... I really want to be accepted as part of the team.

Their Satisfactions...
It's really nice to be recognised by relatives and patients as having done the job well... it makes you feel appreciated after all the effort. I feel that I'm able to help patients' families more now than when I was a student... somehow they seem to respond better to me. You get more recognition as a staff nurse than you did when you were just one of the students... I certainly feel more accepted as a member of the team now than I ever did when I was training... it's really satisfying being able to make decisions rather than having to wait for others to make them for you... I feel now that I am able to stand up for what I feel needs doing... being accountable keeps me on my toes, I like that... people seem to give you more credit as a Registered Nurse.

Things They Wish They'd Known Before Qualifying...
- How to delegate jobs to others, and how not to feel guilty for doing it.
- Assertiveness—how to question others' opinions.
- How to care for bereaved relatives.
- Some career guidance, for example setting career objectives.
- What is available in further education for nurses.
- How to manage time and work better.
- More about legal issues.
- How to use a computer.
- More knowledge about what is available in the community.
- Lateral thinking skills.
- That someone is available for advice.
- Not to worry that what others might be thinking is critical of you.
- How to be more confident.
- How to deal with stress.

Their Advice to the Newly Qualified...
- Remember that you can do it.
- Be assertive; ask for support when you need it.
- Keep in touch with others who are newly qualified, for support.
- Don't be afraid to put your ideas into practice.
- Don't feel guilty when you have to delegate work to others.
- Keep learning and reading.
- Keep informed about career opportunities.
- Make sure that you understand what is expected of you.
- Take your time and don't feel pressured to rush all the time.
- Do what you believe is right at the time.
- Don't be afraid to ask if you are uncertain.
- Remember you are human.

COPING WITH THE CHANGES

The newly qualified staff nurse is sometimes identifiable by an over-confidence, a smugness even, when dealing with students. This type falls soon, and often falls hard. At the other extreme, there is the uncertain, soft-treading novice who seeks reassurance from anyone available at almost every turn. However, the majority quickly settle into a routine of practical confidence which is backed up by a keen interest in their early posts, and later on secured by further study.

From your very first day you will find that people treat you differently, no longer as a student but as a qualified practitioner. Your advice will be sought, both inside and outside work, on a range of health and welfare issues. You can expect to go through a number of changes as you adjust to this new role, which is in effect a new identity. The main change may be the realisation that nursing, for which you have spent three or four years preparing, must sometimes give way to managing the work of others in a clinical area, and liaison with health-care professionals, patients and their relatives—all of which may seem a world away from your chosen profession. If you are lucky your preregistration course will have taken account of your needs as a newly qualified nurse, and will have introduced you to basic managerial skills, both personal and professional. Nevertheless, such changes take time to adjust to, and will call upon your reserves of energy both in your professional and private life.

Self management, very similar to that which you needed as a student, is a top priority. You will need to set aside time to work with, and observe, other more experienced colleagues, not from the perspective of a student, but as a qualified manager of care. Please don't fall into the trap of accepting the practices of others just for the sake of convenience. Be selective in what you choose to take on in your own practice. Bad habits are notoriously difficult to break, so avoid them at the outset.

FOUR RULES FOR THE NEWLY QUALIFIED

- You are now a professional in your own right, and are not there to do the bidding of others, nor to be a handmaiden for doctors, or a general cure-all for anyone else.
- Avoid taking on everything that is offered to you each working day. Learn to say no. If you are one of those nurses who have a martyr instinct, taking on everything and trying to be all things to all people... STOP! You are a human being in a new and challenging situation—you should allow yourself time to reflect on your practice, rather than just getting on with it without thinking.
- Take time to discuss your early work with more experienced colleagues as well as other newly qualified nurses. Take every opportunity to reflect on your work and experiences. This is important and will help you to learn.
- Be gentle with yourself. Don't create impossible goals. Set yourself realistic targets and don't be afraid to ask more experienced colleagues for guidance. You do not have to take their advice, but a little bit of market research never hurt, and they will usually feel flattered by your interest.

The three or four years of your education were a learning experience, and the next three or four will be no less so. Far from being over, your education is just beginning.

GOOD LUCK !

SUMMARY

- Moving from studenthood to the real world may be daunting.
- Be prepared for change.
- Choose jobs carefully; be prepared to move to find a suitable job.
- Make plans, set realistic goals.
- Recognise your limitations.
- Be gentle with yourself.
- Share your concerns with others.
- Remember that this is a new and exciting phase in which you will learn a great deal.

CAREER
OPPORTUNITIES

Part of the attraction of nursing is the immense variety of work available throughout the world. It is possible to work either independently or as a team member, and the choice of clinical or non-clinical work is wide. Nurses are employed in all spheres of life, and the personal and financial rewards are similarly diverse.

It is possible to get stuck in a rut in nursing, just as in any other work, although there is usually some degree of flexibility. There are also opportunities to earn quite large amounts of money (contrary to the popular belief that all nurses are poorly paid). Although riches are not on every doorstep, they do exist; for example, when working in some overseas countries, or on offshore oil rigs, the pay can be very high. Nursing in the USA has enormous earning potential, particularly for those taking on roles such as nurse anaesthetists, where the pay is commensurate with the high level of responsibility and training required. I know of one nursing couple who enjoyed holidays in Europe, a brand new car each year, and whose hobbies included flying helicopters!

This chapter takes a look at some of the opportunities open to the qualified nurse, and considers their advantages and disadvantages. This is by no means an exhaustive account.)

THE NHS AND NURSING PRACTICE
The vast majority of Registered Nurses in the UK are employed by the National Health Service. Most find themselves doing clinical bedside nursing on a hospital ward, or caring in the community. The service has in the past had a well-defined career ladder, which usually involved work as a staff nurse followed by promotion into sister grades. Some nurses went on into teaching or managerial posts. These administrative routes take the nurse away from patients and (arguably) out of nursing, into the type of work experienced by managers in many non-nursing fields.

The work done by most Registered Nurses is, as we have seen, rather different from the idea that most people have on entering their pre-registration programme. Nurses care for patients not only directly. Registered Nurses often supervise care delivery by unqualified staff, such as students and health care assistants. In fact, the clinical grades of staff nurse or sister, with their diverse interests, satisfy most people's nursing ambitions—although they may sometimes aspire to more, many would admit to finding fulfilment in these roles.

The National Health Service has advantages, in that it is relatively easy to transfer within the service to different posts throughout the country. Those with itchy feet have had less difficulty in moving than they might have had in the commercial world.

The introduction of NHS Trusts and self-governed hospitals has significantly altered nurses' career structures and job prospects. For example, many trusts now employ health care assistants, who deliver bedside care under the supervision of Registered Nurses. Health care assistants are paid less than Registered Nurses—this allows the hospitals to reduce their staff costs, but leads to a reduction in the number of jobs available for Registered Nurses, as hospitals attempt to minimise their costs.

Nevertheless, the NHS is still the largest employer of nurses in the UK. Career opportunities remain reasonably good, despite the changes, though there will be fewer opportunities for movement within the service than previously. The future for many Registered Nurses may therefore be with the private sector health care service, which is expanding in the UK as in other countries.

PRIVATE HEALTH CARE

The private sector has grown in recent years, competing with and sometimes supplementing the NHS. Qualified nurses are increasingly moving into this area as opportunities in the NHS disappear.

Nurses working in private hospitals sometimes earn little or no more than their NHS counterparts, although minor perks, such as free meals while on duty, are offered. This contrasts sharply with the huge income enjoyed by doctors working in private health care. Moreover, the commercial ethos of the private sector engenders a different approach to nursing and other health care work. For example, time spent on caring may be reduced, a result of the need to maximise work and profit for the employer. Also, private patients are often nursed in individual rooms—this may seem attractive, but it can lead to loneliness and isolation. The fact that nurses cannot see patients without going into individual rooms is felt by some to be a problem, particularly where a patient needs close observation. (NHS hospitals have fewer individual rooms, patients being accommodated in bays of four or six beds, or larger more open wards.)

Certain specialised areas of care available in the NHS are less widely available in the private sector at present. For example, those with mental health problems might be cared for in an environment which has neither the appropriate staff or the facilities to meet their needs. (This is not always the case. There are private sector and residential homes providing formal care for mental health, mental handicap and elderly client groups, some of them exceedingly well.)

The introduction of the National Health Service and Community Care Act 1990 led to the formation of Trusts and the creation of internal market forces designed to govern the provision of health care. As a result of the changes certain decisions, such as whether people are cared for in local authority or privately run facilities, are influenced by economic considerations. These developments are leading to the establishment of more types of nursing posts, increasing the variety of career opportunities for qualified nurses. Community and hospital liaison nurses will be concerned with people who have been discharged from hospital to be looked after in the community. Developments in the area of child care in the home will be enabled by community-based Children's Liaison Nurses. As local authorities become responsible for the provision of care services, more nurses will be employed by the Family Health Service Authority (FHSA), many in health centre practices.

NURSE TEACHERS

Opportunities to teach nurses are rarer than they used to be. This is due mainly to the changes in the NHS and the consequent reduced demand for qualified nurses. The system of nurse education encompasses colleges of nursing and higher education establishments such as universities.

The Nurse Tutor

To qualify as a nurse tutor in a college of nursing you must have a minimum of three years' recent nursing experience as a Registered Nurse. ('Recent' in this case means 'within seven years of applying to register as a tutor'.) During that time, you must have held a position of responsibility in an area which contained nursing students on clinical placement. For most people this means being employed as a staff nurse or sister. The present system favours graduates, and a degree will be mandatory by the mid-1990s. To teach, therefore, requires an education beyond basic registration level, together with practical nursing experience. In addition to all this, the tutor must complete a Certificate in Education, which confers the status of Qualified Teacher. Following a period of supervised teaching, usually twelve months in a college or similar establishment, the teacher can apply for a place on the register of nurse teachers.

The work of a nurse tutor is very demanding. Although she or he no longer works shifts, this is more than made up for by the long hours spent preparing and marking students' work. Added to this, there is the personal responsibility felt towards students who often share their problems with their tutor—there is rarely time allowed for this in the tutor's working day.

The Nurse Lecturer

Teaching in higher education (HE) establishments, such as universities (including former polytechnics), has slightly different requirements. There is no specified minimum period experience, nor is there a requirement to be on the register of nurse tutors. However, in practice the majority are educated to at least Bachelor degree level, and in most cases to Masters degree level, and have at least as much experience as their nurse-college counterparts. Many HE establishments are also placing added emphasis on the need for lecturers to acquire a teaching qualification. Working as a lecturer means teaching at a higher academic level than a college tutor, and requires a more flexible approach to working hours. You may have to teach in the evenings, and although the holidays may appear attractive, the sheer amount of work in an academic year often spills over into many lecturers' free time.

RESEARCH

Nursing is evolving as a research-based discipline, and the uniqueness of the profession means that it is nurses who carry out research into 'what nurses do'. To facilitate this, a number of research posts have been created within the NHS. Only a few of these posts exist at present, but there is every possibility of more nurses being involved, either full- or part-time, in the future. This is reinforced by the introduction of continuing education requirements for nurses, and the increasing numbers of nurses following part-time degree programmes. In such programmes they are introduced to research as a practice discipline in which they discover the benefits available to nurses and patients alike.

Options for a full-time career in research are limited at present. Nevertheless, research has an essential part to play in the development of the profession.

SPECIALIST COURSES
Midwife

The work of midwives spans a broad area, including hospital and community care for both women and men, before, during and after delivery of their baby. The midwife develops a relationship with the mother-to-be before the estimated due date of birth. She helps with the preparations, teaching about care for both the baby and the new mother. She also helps the mother to become physically and mentally prepared for the delivery. She may arrange attendance at antenatal classes, in which exercises are taught and in which the mother-to-be may be encouraged to ask questions about the whole experience of motherhood.

Midwives see themselves as autonomous and independent practitioners, and strongly defend this separate identity from nursing. Most midwives are highly knowledgeable, and are very much a part of the training of other professionals, for example junior doctors who are allocated to the area for part of their clinical experience.

Midwifery training may be undertaken via two routes. The first is by an eighteen-month post-registration course, following registration as a general nurse. The second option is a three-year full-time course for those who have no nursing background, but who wish to become a midwife directly. Entry requirements are the same as for preregistration courses.

Further details can be obtained through the Nurses and Midwives Central Clearing House, NMCCH (see Appendix, *Useful Addresses*).

Health Visitor

The work of most health visitors is carried out in the community. A few are employed in hospitals, but most are attached to a health centre, where they organise and run clinics, mainly for young families and the elderly. They also visit people's homes and assess their health-care needs. A large part of the health visitor's work is teaching patients about health care, but they also make referrals to other agencies connected with care delivery, for example social services and the general practitioner, as well as the many other agencies and services available to the wider community. The work is considered to be very demanding and frequently stressful, a result of dealing with sometimes very deprived families who may be experiencing traumas, for which they have sought help.

Moves are afoot to allow health visitors to become qualified to prescribe certain medicines and appliances, by taking a short course on the subject. Some see this as an extension of the role of the health visitor, further benefiting the patient, and others as a relief for overloaded doctors.

To qualify as a health visitor, you must first be a Registered Nurse, normally with two years of clinical experience. The health visitor programme lasts one year full time, or two years part time. The courses are normally offered by university departments of nursing.

Qualifications available to health visitors have varied in the past. Some have been at certificate level, but more recent courses have extended to diploma level.

Practice Nurse and District Nurse

Many practice nurses are based at a health centre. The role is currently being developed to cover a wide range of caring activities in the community. They work as health advisors and as monitors of health needs in the wider community. Their work encompasses that of district nurses, who visit patients in their homes and offer follow-up care both from hospital and health centre. Traditionally, the district nurse has helped with dressings on wounds, health care teaching, and assisting the infirm to carry out essential activities such as washing, dressing, feeding and hygiene needs.

Training is open to registered general nurses, and involves attendance at an institution such as a university, usually on a part-time basis for up to one year.

School Nurse

The school nurse, as the name suggests, is responsible for the health care needs of children at school. The work involves visiting schools to carry out routine health checks, as well as visiting children's families to offer advice on children's health needs. The school nurse may also be called in to a school to develop the staff's awareness of the role, and to show how they may contribute towards the identification of actual and potential problems regarding children's health.

Again, training is open to registered general nurses, and involves attendance at an institution such as a university, usually on a part-time basis for up to one year.

Community Psychiatric Nurse

Community psychiatric nurses are responsible for the mental health needs of a group of clients in the community. Their services may be requested through a doctor's referral. Alternatively, patients are followed up after their discharge from hospital. The role of the community psychiatric nurse is becoming increasingly important, as more and more people are cared for in the community. The community psychiatric nurse qualification is available to nurses who have registration in mental health nursing. Qualification usually follows a one-year full-time diploma programme.

Community Nurse For People With Mental Handicap/Learning Difficulties

Community nurses caring for people who have a mental handicap (learning difficulties) have a similar role to that of the community psychiatric nurse. Here a nurse with specialist skills, experience and the appropriate nursing qualification in mental handicap nursing will work with individuals either at home, or in group- or community-based homes.

Occupational Health Nurse

This highly specialised work is usually carried out in commercial and industrial settings, although some occupational health nurses are employed by the NHS. All are based in health centres. The work is broad in scope and includes attendance at accidents, teaching first aid in the workplace, giving advice on health matters, and carrying out immunisations. As well as all this, the nurse needs a good understanding of health and safety legislation. Many of the occupational health nurse's clients need help with personal problems, so counselling skills are also needed. Qualities often considered important for this type of work include: the ability to work unsupervised; very good interpersonal skills; a good listening ear; and assertiveness, to enable the nurse to negotiate with managers and staff at all levels in an organisation. There are opportunities for nurses from this field to work offshore on oil drilling platforms—men are usually employed to work in these male-dominated environments.

Education in occupational health nursing is open to Registered Nurses. Full-time and part-time courses are given by universities and last up to two years.

THE UNIFORMED SERVICES

Registered Nurses are employed in all branches of the uniformed services. Direct entrants normally apply to enter as a commissioned officer. Most contract to serve for two or more years. The hospital-based work is often very similar to that in civilian life, but with the bonus of extra pay and good travel opportunities. Nurses in the armed services enjoy a good deal of variety, living with others who share their sense of adventure. The personality of applicants for such posts is carefully assessed to ensure that they will fit into the system, will be able to tolerate difficult and uncomfortable conditions (e.g. on military exercises), and will be comfortable with the formality associated with military officers.

The army offers positions in the UK at military hospitals and health centres, as well as overseas postings to Continental Europe and the Far East. Some nurses visit areas such as the Falkland Islands or serve on expeditions to (even more) remote parts of the earth. The Royal Air Force has hospital placements in the UK and northern Europe, as well as limited opportunities for specialist training as flight nurses, accompanying patients on flights to and from anywhere in the world. The Royal Navy has nurses both on board ships, and at shore-based hospitals.

As well as the armed services, there are nurses employed in the prison service. There are opportunities to develop a career within the service, and nurses can move between the various prisons throughout the UK.

NURSING OVERSEAS

This applies to nurses registered after 1983, when programmes were expanded to take account of the experience and training normally required in Continental Europe and other overseas countries.

Nurses registered in the UK are frequently sought for work overseas. Agencies advertise in nursing journals and the type of work available varies considerably. Doing voluntary service in the Third World, the living conditions and rate of pay will probably be basic, but the rewards in personal terms enormous. At the other extreme, a job in a wealthy industrialised country like North America will allow a nurse to enjoy a high standard of living in a wide choice of settings. Also, don't forget that European Community regulations permit UK Registered Nurses to practise in any of the member states.

Melanie and David are nurses who have had very different experiences of overseas work:

Melanie In the late 1960s, I undertook my first contract with the 'Save The Children', in Biafra, Nigeria. I was a member of an emergency team of doctors and nurses. There was a war on, and we remained very close to the fighting. Our job was to provide aid to children who were suffering from the disastrous effects of the war. The children suffered from a wide range of illnesses, many of which often proved fatal. The use of tribal or witch-doctor medicine was very common, very ill children sometimes being made to drink stale cows urine as a 'cure'. Needless to say the results were frightful. Working in Third World countries was to be my life for many years, and it was a long time before I could readjust to working as a nurse in England. I would encourage any nurse to work overseas, though everything will be different from what you have been used to. It is essential to be adaptable, flexible, tolerant and open-minded, and you must have a sense of humour. If you think going to work overseas will cure your itchy feet, it won't—you will undoubtedly want to do it again.

David I had only recently qualified as a Registered Nurse when I replied to an advert for work in the USA. The interview took place in a hotel room, the agent being a typical smooth-talking businessman. I had the opportunity of flying out, air fares paid, to work in a plush, modern, private hospital. This was far removed from the cold austerity of England, and the alternative job in a NHS hospital. I flew out after much bureaucratic wrangling over visas and references, to arrive in a very hot climate, knowing no-one. It had been a long flight and my first experience of jet lag, but I had to report for work the next day, and quickly discovered just how hard the nurses had to work—six days a week and only two weeks' holiday after a year in the job! However, the work was interesting and I quickly made friends. The experience was worthwhile, but I wish I had waited a little longer to gain some experience as a qualified nurse before embarking on such a trek. Would I recommend it? Yes, but only after gaining some UK nursing experience first.

Working Overseas—Some Questions Answered

What experience will I need before going?

It is advisable, though not always essential, to obtain one year's experience in the UK before going overseas. This should ensure that you already have some professional competence and confidence before entering a new culture, which in itself may demand a great deal of you. Added to this is the fact that when you come back, you can offer employers the benefits of your previous experience as a staff nurse in the UK system.

What extra training and qualifications will I need?

This depends on where you plan to work.

If you go to Australia, you can usually apply for a reciprocal registration based on your training in the UK. You will need to pay for this—the Australian Embassy will be able to advise you. The process of obtaining visas and registration can take about six months, so be prepared to wait.

To work in the USA you must sit an exam—the Certificate for Graduates of Foreign Nursing Schools (CGFNS)—before you leave the UK. Once you get to the USA you must pass an exam set by the nursing board—there is one for every State—before you can register and practise. (The sole exception to this rule is Arkansas, which is a *beautiful* place.)

Agencies hiring for work in the Third World often seek nurses who are also registered midwives.

How long must I commit myself for?

Many agencies seeking nurses to work overseas insist on a one- or two-year contract.

What if I don't like it?

You will be under contract, and will have to negotiate termination with your employer.

Will I be able to stay on longer?

Many contracts are renewable by mutual consent, and you might be able to negotiate improvements in your conditions based on your record.

What will I need to pay for?

Most agencies do not charge the nurse, but you may have to buy your own uniform and, in some countries, a stethoscope. You will often be expected to pay for your registration and so on. These expenses are normally tax deductible.

Are there any bad points ?

As with any adventure, there are bound to be hardships. These will vary according to your personality and your previous experiences. The problems of living away from home have already been discussed—add to this the change in culture and the inherent difficulties of the place you go to, and yes, there will be some difficulties. In the USA, for example, some places are really wild—sleeping with a loaded pistol beside your bed may take a little getting used to! Countries like Australia, though incredibly beautiful, harbour the world's five most dangerous snakes, and poisonous spiders are found in many a suburban backyard.

What are the good points ?

You will really grow, both in maturity generally, and in your own self-awareness. There is little to equal travel for broadening your outlook on life. The experience will always be with you, and as a nurse you will undoubtedly have an edge on your stay-at-home counterparts. Just ask anyone who has spent time overseas.

SELF-EMPLOYMENT

Most nurses are employed by other people. Other than running a nursing/residential home or nursing agency, there is little opportunity for self-employment for nurses. Some countries—the USA and Australia—have nurse-run health centres, where the Registered Nurses offer a service similar to general practice, calling in a doctor or specialist when they need one. This hasn't taken off in the UK yet, but no doubt it will, given time. Nurses are not permitted to advertise their skills, or to be paid for endorsing commercial products.

SUMMARY

- The world is wide-open with opportunities for nurses.
- The National Health Service in the UK is changing. This will affect nurses' careers. Some will find more opportunities, others will find less. It is essential to plan your career according to your goals and expectations.
- Private health care has been around for a long time, and there are indications that it will grow. Many nurses will seek opportunities to develop their careers within the private sector.
- Non-clinical posts include management and teaching, the opportunities for which are developing in line with other health care changes.
- There are opportunities for specialisation away from the hospital set-up, through district nursing, occupational health, health visiting and community practice.

- There will always be a need for midwives, this being a specialist area developing apart from mainstream nursing.

- Some nurses prefer to take on extra challenges, finding the armed forces as a suitable vehicle for this. Opportunities vary within the armed forces according to demands, and according to the branch (Army, Navy or Air Force).

- Working overseas continues to attract a steady stream of nurses. Some resettle in the UK after a period abroad, while others find more attractions elsewhere. Opportunities in the overseas job market vary. Advice can be sought from the agencies which advertise in the professional press. Care should be exercised when selecting a post, and contracts should be carefully examined.

The world is wide-open with opportunities for nurses...

14

EDUCATION AND ACADEMIA

THE ACADEMIC HIERARCHY

Most courses that a nurse takes have an academic rating (Table 7). All higher-level courses begin at level 1, and then progress to higher levels. Let us consider some examples of the types of courses available to nurses, and their respective places in the hierarchy.

Certificate (Level 1)
Certificate in school nursing.

Diploma (Level 2)
The diploma in nursing.

Bachelor's Degree (Level 3)
The Bachelor's degree (BSc or BA) is often referred to as a first degree. Bachelor's degrees are mostly taught courses.

Bachelor's Degree With Honours
This is a Bachelor's degree which has an extended content, often research-based, upon which the honours classification is based— BSc(Hons), BA(Hons).

Master's Degree
Master's degrees—MA (Master of Arts), MSc (Master of Science) and others—are sometimes referred to as higher degrees. It is possible to be awarded a Master's degree by following a taught course, by doing research, or by following a combination taught/research course.

Doctorate
The PhD (Doctor of Philosophy) is the highest level of academic achievement. The holder of a doctorate has undertaken original research which has contributed new knowledge to the field.

CREDIT ACCUMULATION TRANSFER SCHEME

Levels 1, 2, and 3 in the hierarchy are awarded credit points, which can be accumulated to count towards higher awards. This system is known as the Credit Accumulation Transfer Scheme (CATS).

CATS operates mainly in the universities that were, until quite recently, polytechnics. Students are able to transfer study credits into awards from any of the institutions which participate in the national scheme.

In order to qualify for one of the above credit-rated courses, it is necessary to have accumulated points through studying approved modules on courses involved in the CATS scheme. There are minimum numbers of points needed at each level in order to qualify for an award. Let us consider an example of how a student might obtain a degree through accumulating credit points.

Level 1

The student needs to obtain a total of 120 credits at level 1 (certificate level) by studying either approved modules or a full course. The student is, if successful, awarded a certificate from the institution at which she or he has studied.

This level equates to the old-style (pre-1983) registration courses for nurses. These courses are not considered to have been very academically advanced, so nurses registered before 1983 will find that their registration qualification is valued at 60 credit points at Level 1. In order to be awarded a certificate of study from a higher education institution, a further 60 credit points at level 1 would be required.

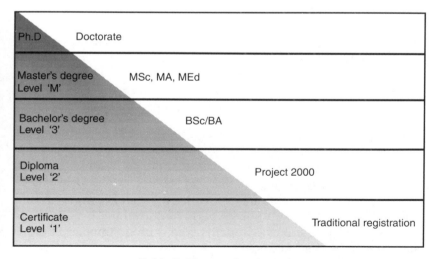

Table 7 The academic scale.

Level 2

Having been successful at level 1, the student can study approved modules or a full course at level 2 (diploma level). Once 120 credit points have been accumulated, a diploma is awarded.

Project 2000 courses qualify the student to diploma level, which illustrates the value given to the qualification in academic terms. A Project 2000 Registered Nurse can qualify for a degree by studying for a further 120 credit points at level 3.

Level 3

This is first-degree level work. The successful student will, on achieving 120 credits at level 3, qualify for the award of a Bachelor's degree. It is possible to continue in this way up to Master's degree level.

ACCREDITATION FOR PRIOR EXPERIENTIAL LEARNING

Many higher education institutions will give students credit for non-academic learning arrived at through experience. For example, someone who has been working in a position of responsibility for a number of years may apply to have credit given against this experiential learning. Institutions consider each case on its own merits.

It may be possible to achieve a certificate by using this prior learning credit towards the required 120 credit points. In practice, an experienced nurse who qualified before 1983 (whose registration is valued at 60 credits) may be able to negotiate up to 60 extra credit points, so reaching full certificate status and qualifying for access to a diploma course.

SPECIFIC AWARDS

It is not possible to qualify for a specific award without undergoing the required learning in that area. For example, no-one can register as a nurse unless they have followed an approved programme specifically for that purpose. It is possible, however, to qualify for a non-specific or general qualification based on a variety of subjects, e.g. a certificate, diploma or degree in combined studies.

THE HIGHER AWARD IN NURSING

This develops through particular study relevant to a nurse's area of practice. The study credits at each level accumulate, and it is possible to reach level 3 (Bachelor's degree) and beyond. The student negotiates areas of learning with her or his manager, and is supervised by an academic in an institution of higher education. There is no set course of study to follow—students plan a programme of study to suit their individual needs, which may involve research as well as study of specific modules on other courses, as appropriate.

POST-REGISTRATION EDUCATION PRACTICE PROJECT

This scheme, known as PREPP, expects all nurses to participate in furthering their education and updating their practice. The scheme involves five days of systematic and recordable participation over three years. It will be mandatory for continued registration.

SUMMARY

- Nursing as an academic discipline is increasing, and the opportunities for development are many and varied.
- It is possible to study nursing as a discipline up to Doctorate level, having first acquired appropriate degrees.
- All nurses will have to demonstrate proof of continuing education.
- More nurses are enrolling on post-registration degree programmes.
- Many nurses will increase their education profile through other, not necessarily nursing-specific, degree and diploma routes.
- Nursing qualifications and experience attract credit ratings through CATS and APEL.

Useful Addresses

Careers Information:

England
English National Board For
   Nursing, Midwifery and Health
   Visiting
Careers Information Centre
PO Box 356
Sheffield S8 OSJ.

Wales
Welsh National Board for Nursing,
   Midwifery and Health Visiting
Floor 13
Pearl Assurance House
Greyfriars Road
Cardiff CF1 3AG.

Scotland
National Board For Nursing,
   Midwifery and Health Visiting for
   Scotland
22 Queen Street
Edinburgh EH2 1JX.

Northern Ireland
National Board For Nursing, Midwifery
   and Health Visiting for Northern Ireland
RAC House
79 Chichester Street
Belfast BT1 4JR.

Application forms for courses are available from:

England
NMCCH
PO Box 346
Bristol BS99 7FB.

Scotland
NBS Catch
PO Box 21
Edinburgh EH2 1NT.

Wales
Apply directly to the college.

Northern Ireland
Same address as above.

For information on management courses:
National Health Service Training Authority
St Bartholomew's Court
18 Christmas Street
Bristol BS1 5BT.

Application forms and information on full time university nursing courses:
University Central Council on Admissions (UCCA)
PO Box 28
Cheltenham
Gloucestershire GL50 1HY.
The Polytechnic Central Admission Service (PCAS) is at the same address.
The two services will combine in 1994.

Armed Services
Careers information may be obtained through the local careers information
offices situated in most major towns. The addresses for these may be found in
the telephone directory. Nursing agencies for local and overseas employment
are listed in the telephone directory. They also advertise in the nursing
journals.

Glossary

ASSESSMENTS Means of gathering information on ability, status, performance.

APEL Assessment of prior experiential learning. Credit given for learning through experience.

BURSARY Money paid to student during course. This is not means tested.

BRANCHES Choice of nursing speciality route.

BACHELOR'S DEGREE A first degree (level 3).

CATS Credit accumulation transfer scheme. Wherein earlier learning/qualifications may be put towards further qualifications.

CNAA Council for National Academic Awards. The governing body of the universities.

CLEARING System whereby applicants without places to study may be considered by other institutions.

CONVERSION From one qualification to another, i.e. enrolled nurse to registered nurse.

COMMON FOUNDATION PROGRAM (CFP) First half of project 2000 course.

CLINICAL Setting in which professional care is practiced.

DOCTORATE A research based degree (PhD).

GRANT A financial award, given to a student in order to finance a course.

HIGHER EDUCATION Education beyond school leaving, normally offering diploma and degree level courses.

HIGHER AWARD A qualification for nurses and midwives, in which the student agrees on a plan of learning with their manager and an educator.

JOURNAL A professional magazine.

MASTERS DEGREE A higher degree awarded by a university or polytechnic.

MYTH A belief existing in a culture or society which may not have any basis in fact.

NATIONAL HEALTH SERVICE (NHS) Begun in 1948 as a health service available to all, regardless of income.

NMCCH Nurses and Midwives Central Clearing House.

PCAS Polytechnic Central Admission System.

PhD Doctorate.

PREPP Post-registration education practice project. A scheme in which all nurses will have to demonstrate updated professional knowledge and competence.

PROJECT 2000 (P2K) A new, student-directed approach to nurse education leading to registration as a nurse.

RGN Registered General Nurse.

RMN Registered Mental Nurse.

RNMH Registered Nurse Mental Handicap/Learning difficulties.

RSCN Registered Sick Children's Nurse.

STEREOTYPE Classing all of a group as the same.

SUPERNUMERARY Not part of the numbered workforce.

TRUST (NHS) Self/locally governed hospitals.

UNDERGRADUATE A student on a first degree course.

UCCA University Central Council for Admissions.

Index